By Mark Guy

A Series of Practical Guides

Choosing a Sperm Donor

Copyright

This edition copyright © 2016 Mark Guy Valerius Tyson

UK

Mark Guy Valerius Tyson asserts the moral right to be identified
as the principal author of this work

MGVT is not liable for any foreseeable or unforeseeable
occurrences resulting from any information given in this
book.

ISBN: 1532941447
ISBN-13: 978-1532941443

EDITED AND SELECTED
BY MARK GUY VALERIUS TYSON

WWWW.MGVT.CO.UK

AUTHORS:

C.W. SALEEBY
P. POPENOE
M.G.V. TYSON

CONTENTS

INTRODUCTION

Whatever your circumstance for choosing a sperm donor, and whether you will call it fate or the will of God, you are in an incredible position. Because, you will be able to give more of a share to thought than to feeling, and you are able to make the best inheritance for your child, your only goal. In this manner, you pass on a great fortune, an estate that cannot be taxed to your future child. Therefore if you choose a poor donor, it is very much like squandering a large inheritance, and it is of great importance that you choose the best donor available to you. It cannot be too strongly emphasised that the information in this book is a statistical law, not a biological law. It must not be applied to predict the character of the offspring of any one particular mating, for it might be highly misleading. It would be wholly unjustified, for example, to suppose that a certain man got three-tenths of his nature from his father, because the Law of Ancestral Heredity required it: in point of fact, he might get one-tenth or nine-tenths, none or all of a given trait. The best you can do is give yourself and your future child the best chance possible, by choosing an appropriate sperm donor, then, to ensure proper health and care during your pregnancy.

If this book inspires in you a taste from genealogy, you may consider purchasing Israel in Britain, a book detailing the ancestry of Europe, America and Asia

God Bless

Mark Guy Valerius Tyson.

A HISTORY OF MENDELIAN INHERITANCE

The contemporary of Charles Darwin, who died without hearing his name, Johann Mendel was only thirteen years younger than Darwin, being born in Silesia in 1822 – the same year as Galton. In 1847 Johann was ordained a priest, assuming the religious name of Gregor. This was at Brünn, and there Mendel passed the rest of his life, except for a visit to Vienna, where he studied science. Teaching was in his family, and he taught so well that this was his monastic work until he was appointed abbot of the monastery of Brünn in 1868.

Mendel's Early Experiments. The young monk had hitherto enjoyed much leisure, which he devoted to botanical and zoological observation. He had the great garden of the cloister at his disposal, and into it he introduced many new plants in order to study their behaviour. Heredity, rather than the effects of nurture upon growth, was his special interest. Especially was he concerned to study the results of mating individuals who were conspicuously different in their personal characteristics.

The foregoing paragraph helps us to understand much about Mendel's work. He was prepared to devote years of labour, of the most arduous and wearisome kind, so much for the quality of the man. But, further, the very nature of his experiments involved their neglect by his contemporaries. To several of these he sent his work, but they were all indifferent to it, thinking it was nothing worthy of mention. But the history of science has shown, over and over again, that the man worked hard shaping the discarded block, which has become the cornerstone of hereditary and genealogy.

Mendel's Many Activities. Mendel, worked at many things, not unworthy of note before we proceed to the great study which now makes him famous. He studied Sun-spots and the weather, and it is known he did much work upon heredity in bees. These insects are of particular interest, seeing that different sexes of offspring are produced according as the ova are fertilised by male cells or not. Further, there are many types of bee, well differentiated; and there ae large possibilities in the direction of improving the yield of honey, and also of removing the power to sting. Mendel had fifty hives in the cloister garden, and collected and studied queen bees from all parts of the world. Nothing whatever remains, of all his labours, but the empty hives. It is probable that he destroyed all his notes before his death, at a time when he was terribly depressed in mind and body. He is another great loss to science which is only now being repaired.

It is recorded that Mendel once remarked that Darwin's theory did not suffice to account for the facts, at the time when the whole world was in a tumult of excitement over Darwin's theory, when it was in fact, Mendel's paper that was the one really substantial and significant new contribution to science. But no one knew that exact and momentous knowledge of heredity, upon which, as we now know, all theories of organic evolution must depend, had been obtained by an obscure monk in Silesia.

The Close of Mendel's Life. The rest of Mendel's life can only too easily be told. When appointed abbot, he hoped that more time for scientific work would be available. God willed otherwise. Here is the account of the facts, given by Professor Bateson:

"In 1872 the government passed a law imposing special taxes on the property of religious houses. This enactment Mendel conceived to be unjust, and he decided to resists, claiming that all citizens should be equal in law, and that if these taxes were imposes on one class of institution they should be imposed on all. He thus took up a position which in England we call a 'passive resister.' At first several other monasteries stood out with him, but gradually they conformed, Mendel alone remaining firm... It is only too certain that the last ten years of his life were passed in disappointment and bitterness. From being a cheerful and friendly man he became suspicious and misanthropic."

Shortly after his death, the tax was removed. It is probable the disease from which he suffered also helped to embitter his mind. In 1882 Darwin died, and in 1884 Mendel followed him, after long ill health, which, as we have seen, probably involved the destruction of some invaluable records.

Not until 1900 did the rediscovery and development of Mendel's discovery begin, to which our next chapter must be devoted. Here our business is to note Mendel's method and carefully to study his results, embodied in what we may call *Mendel's Law or Mendelian Inheritance.*

Three Generations under Observation. What is most important with regard to Mendel's method is the fact that Mendel studied always at least three generations. All inquiries made into the inheritance of particular characteristics, in any species, which confine themselves to the comparison of parents and offspring must be set aside as incomplete. In all such cases we require a complete record of three generations before we have enough material to form any conclusions upon.

That is one of the cardinal reforms in heredity and genetic inquiry which we owe to the patience and thoroughness of Mendel, and it furnishes the condemnation of a great deal of websites, clinics, the NHS, and so-called private sperm donors who have persisted in ignoring Mendel's experience, and in basing supposed laws of heredity upon comparison between parents and offspring only.

Mendel's Precautions. A long familiar fact of heredity

should have sufficed to warn observers that only the record of three consecutive generations could suffice as data for genetic inferences. It has long been noted that features sometimes "skip a generation," as we say, so that a child resembles a grandparent in some character that the parent does not show at all. Yet, of course, that character must have been transmitted by the parent, in whom it must have been latent. Clearly these such cases must not be viewed as freaks or eccentricities. Clearly we must study the third generation in every case, for in it we may find the reappearance of striking characteristics which were absent from the individuals of the first filial generation, and of which, if our study had ended with them, we should say that they were not inherited.

This was exactly what Mendel regularly found, thanks to the fact that his method was the right one: certain types of inherited characteristics technically called "recessives," **must** disappear in the first generation, under certain conditions, and must as surely reappear in the second.

Results of the first mating. When the tall and short peas were mated, all the offspring were always tall – as tall as the tall parent. That fact in itself is remarkable, in such a case we would have expected "blended inheritance," and expect to find the offspring about three feet high – a compromise between the stature of their parents. Such a compromise is what we seem to find when dark and white skinned people mate. But in the case the peas it looked as if the tallness was inherited and the shortness was not. The sex of the tall and short parents respectively did not alter the result.

Remarkable results of the continued experiment. The next task was to mate these all-tall members of the first filial generation with each other. Had they been tall plants of a normal kind with nothing but tallness in their ancestry, of course all the offspring would have been tall also. This did not happen. When huge numbers were counted, it was found that, with strict regularity, 75% of the second filial generation were tall, but the remaining 25% were dwarfs, like their one dwarf grandparent. This shortness had "skipped a generation."

Instead of talking percentages, let us talk in strict numbers. We now have three tall plants and one short to deal with. The first and simplest fact is that the short ones, when bred together, yield nothing but short offspring, generation to generation. Clearly there is no tallness in them, visible or invisible, patent or latent, though both their parents were tall. But of the remaining three plants, distinctions must be made. One of them, like the one short plant, when tested, is found to be a pure tall, like the original tall grandparent. Such plants mated together produce nothing but tall, generation after generation. The remaining two tall plants, however behave exactly like their own parents, again yielding offspring in the proportion of three tall to one short.

Dominant and Recessive Characters. These are the facts which Mendel ascertained; and what is true for tallness and shortness is also for various other contrasted pairs of characteristics. Now, it is clear that the character tallness has the power to assert itself over the character shortness, even though that be also present as the results of further breeding proves.

Mendel, therefore, gave the name *dominant* to characteristics which behave as tallness does; and the opposite character, which recedes in the presence of the dominant, Mendel called a recessive. If the dominant character is present, usually it asserts itself.

Segregation, the Basis of Mendel's Theory. Clearly we must form a new conception of all living individuals who are derived, as nearly all are, from two parents. Every such individual is in a true sense a double thing, as its history teaches us. Before we can understand it, or predict the nature of its offspring, we must be acquainted with what comes to it from both its parents, grandparents and great grand-parents; and the central fact which Mendel discovered is that the respective parental contributions are not necessarily blended in the individual, but remain independent in this sense that they may be passed on separately. This is the central fact of *segregation* upon which Mendelian Inheritance is based.

How the Experiments Bear on the Study of Heredity. Mendel himself did not go at all into theory, but simply described the facts. He looked upon a dominant and recessive as contrasted factors, and offered no explanation either of their nature in themselves nor of the curious way in which they are opposed to each other, nor of the reason why there should be this relation between them, that, though they are both equal in other respects, one dominates the other when both are present in one individual. The lessons which we immediately learn from Mendel's experiments are evident.

Mendelism Applies to Man. The final point that needs to be made in tracing Mendelian studies, is that they are now known to be relevant – not merely to animals as well as plants, but to Man as well. An argument was advanced that, the relatively simple case of colour, Mendelism did not apply to man, for when black and white are mated the offspring are of 'mixed race', a blend of, or compromise between the parents, and show no sign of Mendelian Segregation.

Skin and Hair Colouring. But, in fact, this criticism was far too hasty, and omitted to inquire carefully into the offspring of such parents, when mated among themselves. This particular case is not simple and depends on, as in so many other cases, more than one factor, but clear observation and intuition solves this on Mendelian lines. Certain characteristics of hair-colour, and of the form of the hairs – straight or 'fizzy' – and right and left handedness, practically complete the list of *normal* Mendelian characters in man. We are aware of cases where blonde hair is a dominant character in some instances and a recessive character in others. Characteristics such as these are only determined by breeding, if blonde hair persists in the family despite the introduction of black hair, then we can say with some measure of accuracy that this type of blonde hair is a dominant character.

Desirable Traits, Disease and Heredity. Here we see the very practical value of Mendelism. There are many forms of desirable traits, such as intelligence, strength and hair colour, defects, disease or susceptibility to disease, such as deafness, colour blindness, feeble-mindness and a list of scores besides, in man. Suppose we do or do not want a certain character in our future child, without our Mendelian key, we might be helpless in such a case. One might just choose a donor based only on information about the potential parent, without knowing his desirable or deplorable family history, but this problem is now soluble. First we must look to the records and note whether the desirable or undesirable trait occurs within the last three generations to at least the great grandparent. If the trait appears to be dominant or recessive it will reappear in the offspring of individuals possessing it, in various proportions which we have already outlined. Recent inquiries into musical faculty suggest that this trait is a recessive much like other types of nervous diease. The immense practical importance of such a discovery as this can scarcely be overstated.

The Marriage of Cousins. As a character may be recessive, it follows that, according to the constitution of the parents, *normal* offspring may be carrying the recessive character in their germ cells. The prejudice against cousin marriages merely means that if, and only if, the constitution of the parents be affected by a bad trait, any offspring will have a one in four chance of developing this undesirable trait. But, on the other hand, if the recessive character is a desirable one, such a cousin marriage may yield one child in four possessing the welcome trait, though neither parent had it patently. Does this not throw an entirely new light upon the problem of marriage of relations? At once we see that the simplest and truest answer to inquiries as to the consequence of marriages between cousins is that it depends on the cousin.

The Significance of Mendel's Discovery. We must absolutely clear our minds, of any assumption that dominant and recessive have anything to do with desirable or undesirable, normal or abnormal characters. Each case has to be worked out empirically and dealt with according to the result found. Lastly, in this connection we note that a normal woman considering having a baby by sperm donor, who belonging to a family which is affected by some undesirable recessive trait may either be free of it or may carry it, and for the best chance of having a child that is free from all undesirable characters, it is best to make sure that the chosen donor has no history of this trait for at least as far back as the great grandparents, which otherwise, might prove highly disastrous.

MARK TYSON - C.W. SALEEBY

NATURE OR NURTURE

It is widely supposed that, although nature may have distributed some handicaps at birth, they can be removed if the body is properly warmed and fed and the mind properly exercised. It is further widely supposed that this improvement in the condition of the individual will result in his production of better infants, and that thus the race, gaining a little momentum in each generation, will gradually move on toward ultimate perfection.

There is no lack of efforts to improve children, by this method of direct change of the environment. It involves two assumptions, which are sometimes made explicitly, sometimes merely taken for granted. These are:

That changes in a man's surroundings, or, to use the more technical biological term, in his nurture, will change the nature that he has inherited.

That such changes will further be transmitted to his children.

Galton adopted and popularised Shakespeare's antithesis of nature and nurture to describe a man's inheritance and his surroundings, the two terms including everything that can pertain to a human being. The words are not wholly suitable, particularly since nature has two distinct meanings,--human nature and external nature. The first is the only one considered by Galton. Further, nurture is capable of subdivision into those environmental influences which do not undergo much change,--e.g., soil and climate,--and those forces of civilisation and education which might better be described as culture. The evolutionist has really to deal with the three factors of germ-plasm, physical surroundings and culture. But Galton's phrase is so widely current that we shall continue to use it, with the implications that have just been outlined.

The antithesis of nature and nurture is not a new one; it was met long ago by biologists and settled by them to their own satisfaction. The whole body of experimental and observational evidence in biology tends to show that the characters which the individual inherits from his ancestors remain remarkably constant in all ordinary conditions to which they may be subjected. Their constancy is roughly proportionate to the place of the animal in the scale of evolution; lower forms are more easily changed by outside influence, but as one ascends to the higher forms, which are more differentiated, it is found more and more difficult to effect any change in them. Their characters are more definitely fixed at birth.

It is with the highest of all forms, Man, which we have now to deal. The student in biology is not likely to doubt that the differences in men are due much more to inherited nature than to any influences brought to bear after birth, even though these latter influences include such powerful ones as nutrition and education within ordinary limits.

But the biological evidence does not lend itself readily to summary treatment, and we shall therefore examine the question by statistical methods. These have the further advantage of being more easily understood; the problem of nature vs. nurture cannot be solved in general terms; a moment's thought will show that it can be understood only by examining one trait at a time. The problem is to decide whether the differences between the people met in everyday life are due more to inheritance or to outside influences, and these differences must naturally be examined separately; they cannot be lumped together.

To ask whether nature in general contributes more to a

man than nurture is futile; but it is not at all futile to ask whether the differences in a given human trait are more affected by differences in nature than by differences in nurture. It is easy to see that a verdict may be sometimes given to one side, sometimes to the other. Albinism in animals, for instance, is a trait which is known to be inherited, and which is very slightly affected by differences of climate, food supply, etc. On the other hand, there are factors which, although having inherited bases, owe their expression almost wholly to outside influences. Professor Morgan, for example, has found a strain of fruit flies whose offspring in cold weather are usually born with supernumerary legs. In hot weather they are practically normal. If this strain were bred only in the tropics, the abnormality would probably not be noticed; on the other hand, if it were bred only in cold regions, it would be set down as one characterised by duplication of limbs. The heredity factor would be the same in each case, the difference in appearance being due merely to temperature.

Mere inspection does not always tell whether some feature of an individual is more affected by changes in heredity or changes in surroundings. On seeing a swarthy man, one may suppose that he comes of a swarthy race, or that he is a fair-skinned man who has lived long in the desert. In the one case the swarthiness would be inheritable, in the other not. Which explanation is correct, can only be told by examining a number of such individuals under critical conditions, or by an

examination of the ancestry. A man from a dark-skinned race would become little darker by living under the desert sun, while a white man would take on a good deal of tan.

The limited effect of nurture in changing nature is in some fields a matter of common observation. The man who works in the gymnasium knows that exercise increases the strength of a given group of muscles for a while, but not indefinitely. There comes a time when the limit of a man's hereditary potentiality is reached, and no amount of exercise will add another milli-meter to the circumference of his arm. Similarly the handball or tennis player someday reaches his highest point, as do

runners or race horses. A parallel case is found in the students who take a college examination. Half a dozen of them may have devoted the same amount of time to it-- may have crammed to the limit--but they will still receive widely different marks. These commonplace cases show that nurture has seemingly some power to mold the individual, by giving his inborn possibilities a chance to express themselves, but that nature says the first and last word. Francis Galton hit on an ingenious and more convincing illustration by studying the history of twins.

There are, everyday observation shows, two kinds of twins--ordinary twins and the so-called identical twins. Ordinary twins are merely brothers, or sisters, or brother and sister, who happen to be born two at a time, because two ova have developed simultaneously. The fact that they were born at the same time does not make them alike-- they differ quite as widely from each other as ordinary brothers and sisters do. Identical twins have their origin in a different phenomenon--they are believed to be halves of the same egg-cell, in which two growing-points appeared at a very early embryonic stage, each of these developing into a separate individual. As would be expected, these identical twins are always of the same sex, and extremely like each other, so that sometimes their own mother cannot tell them apart. This likeness extends to all sorts of traits:--they have lost their milk teeth on the same day in one case, they even fell ill on the same day with the same disease, even though they were in different cities.

Galton reasoned that if environment really changes the

inborn character, then these identical twins, who start life as halves of the same whole, ought to become more unlike if they were brought up apart; and as they grew older and moved into different spheres of activity, they ought to become measurably dissimilar. On the other hand, ordinary twins, who start dissimilar, ought to become more alike when brought up in the same family, on the same diet, among the same friends, with the same education. If the course of years shows that identical twins remain as like as ever and ordinary twins as unlike as ever, regardless of changes in conditions, then environment will have failed to demonstrate that it has any great power to modify one's inborn nature in these traits.

With this view, Galton collected the history of eighty pairs of identical twins, thirty-five cases being accompanied by very full details, which showed that the twins were really as nearly identical, in childhood, as one could expect to find. On this point, Galton's inquiries were careful, and the replies satisfactory. They are not, however, as he remarks, much varied in character. "When the twins are children, they are usually distinguished by ribbons tied around the wrist or neck; nevertheless the one is sometimes fed, physicked, and whipped by mistake for the other, and the description of these little domestic catastrophes was usually given by the mother, in a phraseology, that is sometimes touching by reason of its seriousness. I have one case in which a doubt remains whether the children were not changed in their bath, and the presumed A is not really B, and vice versa. In another case, an artist was engaged on the portraits of twins who were between three and four years of age; he had to lay aside his work for three weeks, and, on resuming it, could not tell to which child the respective likeness he had in hand belonged. The mistakes become less numerous on the part of the mother during the boyhood and girlhood of the twins, but are almost as frequent as before on the part of strangers. I have many instances of tutors being unable to distinguish their twin pupils. Two girls used regularly to impose on their music teacher when one of them wanted a whole holiday; they had their lessons at separate hours, and the one girl sacrificed herself to receive two lessons on the same day, while the other one enjoyed herself from morning to evening. Here is a brief and comprehensive account: 'Exactly alike in all, their schoolmasters could never tell them apart; at dancing parties they constantly changed partners without discovery; their close resemblance is scarcely diminished by age."

Not a single case was found in which originally dissimilar characters became assimilated, although submitted to exactly the same influences. Reviewing the evidence in his usual cautious way, Galton declared, "There is no escape from the conclusion that nature prevails enormously over nurture, when the differences of nurture do not exceed what is commonly to be found among persons of the same rank in society and in the same country."

This kind of evidence was a good start for mendelian inheritance but as the science grew, it outgrew such evidence. It no longer wanted to be told, no matter how minute the details, that "nature prevails enormously over nurture." It wanted to know exactly how much. It refused to be satisfied with the statement that a certain quantity was large; it demanded that it be measured or weighed. So Galton, Karl Pearson and other mathematicians devised means of doing this, and then Professor Edward L. Thorndike of Columbia University took up Galton's problem again, with more refined methods.

The tool used by Professor Thorndike was the coefficient of correlation, which shows the amount of resemblance or association between any two things that are capable of measurement, and is expressed in the form of a decimal fraction somewhere between 0 and the unit 1. Zero shows that there is no constant resemblance at all between the two things concerned,--that they are wholly independent of each other, while 1 shows that they are completely dependent on each other, a condition that rarely exists, of course. For instance, the correlation between the right and left femur in man's legs is .98.

Professor Thorndike found in the New York City schools fifty pairs of twins of about the same age and measured the closeness of their resemblance in eight physical characters, and also in six mental characters, the latter being measured by the proficiency with which the subjects performed various tests. Then children of the same age and sex, picked at random from the same schools, were measured in the same way. It was thus possible to tell how much more alike twins were than ordinary children in the same environment. "If now these resemblances are due to the fact that the two members of any twin pair are treated alike at home, have the same parental models, attend the same school and are subject in general to closely similar environmental conditions, then (1) twins should, up to the age of leaving home, grow more and more alike, and in our measurements the twins 13 and 14 years old should be much more alike than those 9 and 10 years old. Again (2) if similarity in training is the cause of similarity in mental traits, ordinary fraternal pairs not over four or five years apart in age should show a resemblance somewhat nearly as great as twin pairs, for the home and school condition of a pair of the former will not be much less similar than those of a pair of the latter. Again, (3) if training is the cause, twins should show greater resemblance in the case of traits much subject to training, such as ability in addition or multiplication, than in traits less subject to training, such as quickness in marking off the A's on a sheet of printed capitals, or in writing the opposites of words."

The data were elaborately analysed from many points of view. They showed (1) that the twins 12-14 years old were not any more alike than the twins 9-11 years old, although they ought to have been, if environment has great power to mold the character during these so-called "plastic years of childhood." They showed (2) that the resemblance between twins was two or three times as great as between ordinary children of the same age and sex, brought up under similar environment. There seems to be no reason, except heredity, why twins should be more alike. The data showed

(3) that the twins were no more alike in traits subject to much training than in traits subject to little or no training. Their achievement in these traits was determined by their heredity; training did not measurably alter these hereditary potentialities.

"The facts," Professor Thorndike wrote, "are easily, simply and completely explained by one simple hypothesis; namely, that the nature of the germ-cells--the conditions of conception--cause whatever similarities and differences exist in the original natures of men, that these conditions influence mind and body equally, and that in life the differences in modification of mind and body produced by such differences as obtained between the environments of present-day New York City public school children are slight."

"The inferences," he says, "with respect to the enormous importance of original nature in determining the behaviour and achievements of any man in comparison with his fellows of the same period of civilisation and conditions of life are obvious. All theories of human life must accept

as a first principle the fact that human beings at birth

differ enormously in mental capacities and that these differences are largely due to similar differences in their ancestry. All attempts to change human nature must accept as their most important condition the limits set by original nature to each individual."

The extent to which the intelligence of school children is dependent on defective physique and unfavourable home environment is an important practical question, if we wanted to find out whether the healthy children were the most intelligent. One is constantly hearing stories of how the intelligence of school children has been improved by some treatment which improved their general health, but these stories are rarely presented in such a way as to contribute evidence of scientific value. It was desirable to know what exact measurement would show. The intelligence of all the children in fourteen schools was measured in its correlation with weight and height, conditions of clothing and teeth, state of nutrition, cleanliness, good hearing, and the condition of the cervical glands, tonsils and adenoids. It could not be found that mental capacity was closely related to any of the characters dealt with. The particular set of characters measured was taken because it happened to be furnished by data collected for another purpose; the various items are suggestive rather than directly conclusive. Here again, the correlation in most cases was less than .1, as compared with the general heredity correlation of .5.

The investigation need not be limited to problems of bad breeding. Mendelian inheritance, as its name shows, is primarily interested in "good breeding;" it is particularly worthwhile, therefore, to examine the relations between heredity and environment in the production of mental and moral superiority.

If success in life--the kind of success that is due to

great mental and moral superiority--is due to the opportunities a man has, then it ought to be pretty evenly distributed among all persons who have had favourable opportunities, provided a large enough number of persons be taken to allow the laws of probability full play. England offers a good field to investigate this point, because Oxford and Cambridge, her two great universities, turn out most of the eminent men of the country, or at least have done so until recently. If nothing more is necessary to ensure a youth's success than to give him a first-class education and the chance to associate with superior people, then the prizes of life ought to be pretty evenly distributed among the graduates of the two universities, during a period of a century or two.

This is not the case. When we look at the history of England, as Galton did nearly half a century ago, we find success in life to an unexpected degree a family affair. The distinguished father is likely to have a distinguished son, while the son of two "nobodies" has a very small chance of becoming distinguished. To cite one concrete case, Galton found that the son of a distinguished judge had about one chance in four of becoming himself distinguished, while the son of a man picked out at random from the population had about one chance in 4,000 of becoming similarly distinguished.

The objection at once occurs that perhaps social opportunities might play the predominant part; that the son of an obscure man never gets a chance, while the son of the prominent man is pushed forward regardless of his inherent abilities. This, as Galton argued at length, cannot be true of men of really eminent attainments. The true genius, he thought, frequently succeeds in rising despite great obstacles, while no amount of family pull will succeed in making a mediocrity into a genius, although it may land him in some high and very comfortable official position. Galton found a good illustration in the papacy, where during many centuries it was the custom for a pope to adopt one of his nephews as a son, and push him forward in every way. If opportunity were all that is required, these adopted sons ought to have reached eminence as often as a real son would have done; but statistics show that they reached eminence only as often as would be expected for nephews of great men, whose chance is notably less, of course, than that of sons of great men, in whom the intensity of heredity is much greater.

Transfer the inquiry to America, and it becomes even more conclusive, for this is supposed to be the country of equal opportunities, where it is a popular tradition that every boy has a chance to become president. Success may be in some degree a family affair in caste-ridden England; is it possible that the past history of the United States should show the same state of affairs?

Galton found that about half of the great men of England had distinguished close relatives. If the great men of America have fewer distinguished close relatives, environment will be able to make out a plausible case: it will be evident that in this continent of boundless opportunities the boy with ambition and energy gets to the top, and that this ambition and energy do not depend on the kind of family he comes from.

Frederick Adams Woods has made precisely this investigation. The first step was to find out how many eminent men there are in American history. Biographical dictionaries list about 3,500, and this number provides a sufficiently unbiased standard from which to work. Now, Dr. Woods says, if we suppose the average person to have as many as twenty close relatives--as near as an uncle or a grandson--then computation shows that only one person in 500 in the United States has a chance to be a near relative of one of the 3,500 eminent men--provided it is purely a matter of chance. As a fact, the 3,500 eminent men listed by the biographical dictionaries are related to each other not as one in 500, but as one in five. If the more celebrated men alone be considered, it is found that the percentage increases so that about one in three of them has a close relative who is also distinguished. This ratio increases to more than one in two when the families of the forty-six Americans in the Hall of Fame are made the basis of study. If all the eminent relations of those in the Hall of Fame are counted, they average more than one apiece. Therefore, they are from five hundred to a thousand times as much related to distinguished people as the ordinary mortal is.

To look at it from another point of view, something like 1% of the population of the country is as likely to produce a man of genius as is all the rest of the population put together,--the other 99%.

This might still be due in some degree to family influence, to the prestige of a famous name, or to educational advantages afforded the sons of successful men. Dr. Woods' study of the royal families of Europe is more decisive.

In the latter group, the environment must be admitted--on the whole--to be uniformly favourable. It has varied, naturally, in each case, but speaking broadly it is certain that all the members of this group have had the advantage of a good education, of unusual care and attention. If such things affect achievement, then the achievements of this class ought to be pretty generally distributed among the whole class. If opportunity is the cause of a man's success, then most of the members of this class ought to have succeeded, because to every one of royal blood, the door of opportunity usually stands open. One would expect the heir to the throne to show a better record than his younger brothers, however, because his opportunity to distinguish himself is naturally greater. This last point will be discussed first. Dr. Woods divided all the individuals in his study into ten classes for intellectuality and ten for morality, those most deficient in the qualities being put in class 1, while the men and women of preëminent intellectual and moral worth were put in class 10. Now if preëminent intellect and morality were at all linked with the better chances that an inheritor of succession has, then heirs to the throne ought to be more plentiful in the higher grades than in the lower. Actual count shows this not to be the case. A slightly larger percentage of inheritors is rather to be found in the lower grades. The younger sons have made just as good a showing as the sons who succeeded to power; as one would expect if intellect and morality are due largely to heredity,

but as one would not expect if intellect and morality are due largely to outward circumstances.

Are "conditions of turmoil, stress and adversity" strong forces in the production of great men, as has often been claimed? There is no evidence from facts to support that view. In the case of a few great commanders, the times seemed particularly favourable. Napoleon, for example, could hardly have been Napoleon had it not been for the French revolution. But in general there have been wars going on during the whole period of modern European history; there have always been opportunities for a royal hero to make his appearance; but often the country has called for many years in vain. Circumstances were powerless to produce a great man and the nation had to wait until heredity produced him. Spain has for several centuries been calling for genius in leadership in some lines; but in vain. England could not get an able man from the Stuart line, despite her need, and had to wait for William of Orange, who was a descendant of a man of genius, William the Silent. "Italy had to wait fifty years in bondage for her deliverers, Cavour, Garibaldi and Victor

Emmanuel."

"The upshot of it all," Dr. Woods decides, "is that, as regards intellectual life, environment is a totally inadequate explanation. If it explains certain characters in certain instances, it always fails to explain many more, while heredity not only explains all, or at least 90%, of the intellectual side of character in practically every instance, but does so best when questions of environment are left out of discussion."

Despite the good environment almost uniformly present, the geniuses in royalty are not scattered over the surface of the pedigree chart, but form isolated little groups of closely related individuals. One centers in Frederick the Great, another in Queen Isabella of Spain, a third in William the Silent, and a fourth in Gustavus Adolphus. Furthermore, the royal personages who are conspicuously low in intellect and morality are similarly grouped. Careful study of the circumstances shows nothing in the environment that would produce this grouping of genius, while it is exactly what a knowledge of heredity leads one to expect.

In the next place, do the superior members of royalty have proportionately more superior individuals among their close relatives, as was found to be the case among the Americans in the Hall of Fame? A count shows at once that they do. The first six grades all have about an equal number of eminent relatives, but grade 7 has more while grade 8 has more than grade 7, and the geniuses of grade 10 have the highest proportion of nearer relatives of their own character. Surely it cannot be supposed that a relative of a king in grade 8 has on the average a much less favourable environment than a relative of a king in grade 10. Is it not fair, then, to assume that this relative's greater endowment in the latter case is due to heredity?

Conditions are the same, whether males or females be considered. The royal families of Europe offer a test case because for them the environment is nearly uniformly favourable. A study of them shows great mental and moral differences between them, and critical evidence indicates that these differences are largely due to differences in heredity. Differences of opportunity do not appear to be largely responsible for the achievements of the individuals.

We need not stop with the conclusion that equality of training or opportunity is unable to level the inborn differences between men. We can go even farther, and produce evidence to show that equality of training increases the differences in results achieved. This evidence is obtained by measuring the effects of equal amounts of exercise of a function upon individual differences in respect to efficiency in it. Suppose one should pick out, at random, eight children, and let them do problems in multiplication for 10 minutes. After a number of such trials, the three best might average 39 correct solutions in the 10 minutes, and the three poorest might average 25 examples. Then let them continue the work, until each one of them has done 700 examples. Here is equality in training; does it lead to uniform results? Dr. Starch made the actual test which we have outlined and found that the three best pupils gained on the average 45 in the course of doing 700 examples; while the three poorest gained only 26 in the same course of time.

Similar tests have been made of school children in a number of instances, and have shown that equality of training fails to bring about equality of performance. All improve to some extent; but those who are naturally better than their comrades usually become better still, when conditions for all are the same. E. L. Thorndike gives the following tabular statement of a test he conducted:

THE EFFECT OF EQUAL AMOUNTS OF PRACTICE UPON INDIVIDUAL DIFFERENCES IN THE MENTAL MULTIPLICATION OF A THREE-PLACE BY A THREE-PLACE NUMBER

	Amount done per unit of time			Percentage of correct figures in answers		
	Hours of Practice	First 5 Examples	Last 5 or 10 Examples Gain	First 5 Examples	Last 5 or 10 Examples Gain	
Initial highest five individuals	5.1	85	147	61	70	78	18
Initial next five individuals	5.1	56	107	51	68	78	10
Initial next six individuals	5.3	46	68	22	74	82	8
Initial next six individuals	5.4	38	46	8	58	70	12
Initial next five individuals	5.2	31	57	26	47	67	20
Initial next one individual	5.2	19	32	13	100	82	-18

Similar results have been obtained by half a dozen other experimenters, using the tests of mental multiplication, addition, marking A's on a printed sheet of capitals, and the like. It would be a mistake to conclude too much from experiments of such restricted scope; but they all agree in showing that if every child were given an equal training, the differences in these traits would nevertheless be very great.

We are driven back to the same old conclusion, that it is primarily inborn nature which causes the achievements of men and women to be what they are. Good environment, opportunity, training, will give good heredity a chance to express itself; but they cannot produce greatness from bad heredity.

MODIFICATION OF THE GERM-PLASM

Every living creature was at some stage of its life nothing more than a single cell. It is generally known that human beings result from the union of an egg-cell and a sperm-cell, but it is not so universally understood that these germ-cells are part of a continuous stream of germ-plasm which has been in existence ever since the appearance of life on the globe, and which is destined to continue in existence as long as life remains on the globe.

Early investigators tended naturally to look on the germ-cells as a product of the body. Being supposedly products of the body, it was natural to think that they would in some measure reproduce the character of the body which created them; and Darwin elaborated an ingenious hypothesis to explain how the various characters could be represented in the germ-cell. The idea held by him, in common with most other thinkers of his period, is still held more or less unconsciously by those who have not given particular attention to the subject. Generation is conceived as a direct chain: the body produces the germ-cell which produces another body which in turn produces another germ-cell, and so on. But a generation ago this idea fell under suspicion. August Weismann, professor of zoology in the University of Freiburg, Germany, made himself the champion of the new idea, about 1885, and developed it so effectively that it is now a part of the creed of nearly every biologist. Weismann caused a general abandonment of the idea that the germ-cell is produced by the body in each generation, and popularised the conception of the germ-cell as a product of a stream of undifferentiated germ-plasm, not only continuous but (potentially at least) immortal. The body does not produce the germ-cells, he pointed out; instead, the germ-cells produce the body.

The basis of this theory can best be understood by a brief consideration of the reproduction of very simple organisms.

"Death is the end of life," is the belief of many other persons than the Lotus Eaters. It is commonly supposed that everything which lives must eventually die. But study of a one-celled animal, an Infusorian, for example, reveals that when it reaches a certain age it pinches in two, and each half becomes an Infusorian in all appearance identical with the original cell. Has the parent cell then died? It may rather be said to survive, in two parts. Each of these daughter cells will in turn go through the same process of reproduction by simple fission, and the process will be continued in their descendants. The Infusorian can be called potentially immortal, because of this method of reproduction. The immortality, as Weismann pointed out, is not of the kind attributed by the Greeks to their gods, who could not die because no wound could destroy them. On the contrary, the Infusorian is extremely fragile, and is dying by millions at every instant; but if circumstances are favourable, it can live on; it is not inevitably doomed to die sooner or later, as is Man. "It dies from accident often, from old age never." Now the single-celled Infusorian is in many respects comparable with the single-celled germ of the higher animals. The analogy has often been carried too far; yet it remains indisputable that the germ-cells of men reproduce in the same way--by simple fission--as the Infusorian and other one-celled animals and plants, and that they are organised on much the same plan. Given favourable circumstances, the germ-cell should be expected to be equally immortal. Does it ever find these favourable circumstances?

The investigations of microscopists indicate that it does--that evolution has provided it with these favourable circumstances, in the bodies of the higher animals. Let us recall in outline the early history of the fertilised germ-cell, the zygote formed by the union of ovum and spermatozoon (the mature motile male sex cell of an animal, by which the ovum is fertilised, typically having a compact head and one or more long flagella for swimming.) These two unite to form a single cell, which is essentially the same, physiologically, as other germ-cells. It divides in two similar cells; these each divide; the resulting cells again divide, and so the process continues, until the whole body--a fully developed man,--has been produced by division and redivision of the one zygote. But the germ-cell is obviously different from most of the cells that make up the finished product, the body. The latter are highly differentiated and specialised for different functions-- blood cells, nerve cells, bone cells, muscle cells, and so on, each a single cell but each adapted to do a certain work, for which the original, undifferentiated germ-cell was wholly unfit. It is evident that differentiation began to take place at some point in the series of divisions, that is to say, in the development of the embryo.

Theodor Boveri, studying the development of a threadworm, made the interesting discovery that this differentiation began at the first division. Of the two daughter-cells produced from the zygote, one continued dividing at a very slow rate, and without showing any specialisation. Its "line of descent" produced only germ-cells. The products of division of the other daughter-cell began to differentiate, and soon formed all the necessary kinds of cells to make up the body of the mature worm. In this body, the cells from the first daughter-cell mentioned were inclosed, still undifferentiated: they formed the germ-cells of the next generation, and after maturity were ready to be ejected from the body, and to form new threadworms.

Imagine this process taking place through generation after generation of threadworms, and one will realise that the germ-plasm was passed on directly from one generation to the next; that in each generation it gave rise to body-plasm, but that it did not at any time lose its identity or continuity, a part of the germ-plasm being always set aside, undifferentiated, to be handed on to the next generation.

In the light of this example, one can better understand the definition of germ-plasm as "that part of the substance of the parents which does not die with them, but perpetuates itself in their offspring." By bringing his imagination into play, the reader will realise that there is no limit to the backward continuity of this germ-plasm in the threadworm. Granted that each species has arisen by evolution from some other, this germ-cell which is observed in the body of the threadworm, must be regarded as part of what may well be called a stream of germ-plasm, that reaches back to the beginning of life in the world. It will be equally evident that these is no foreordained limit to the forward extension of the stream. It will continue in some branch, as long as there are any threadworms or descendants of threadworms in the world.

The reader may well express doubt as to whether what has been demonstrated for the threadworm can be demonstrated for the higher animals, including man. It must be admitted that in many of these animals conditions are too unfavourable, and the process of embryology too complicated, or too difficult to observe, to permit as distinct a demonstration of this continuity of the germ-plasm, wherever it is sought. But it has been demonstrated in a great many animals; no facts which impair the theory have been discovered; and biologists therefore feel perfectly justified in generalising and declaring the continuity of germ-plasm to be a law of the world of living things.

Focusing attention on its application to man, one sees that the race must represent an immense network of lines of descent, running back through a vast number of different forms of gradually diminishing specialisation, until it comes to a point where all its threads merge in one knot--the single cell with which it may be supposed that life on this globe began. Each individual is not only figuratively, but in a very literal sense, the carrier of the heritage of the whole race—of the whole past, indeed. Each individual is temporarily the custodian of part of the "stuff of life"; from an evolutionary point of view, he may be said to have been brought into existence, primarily to pass this sacred heritage on to the next generation. From Nature's standpoint, he is of little use in the world, his existence is scarcely justified, unless he faithfully discharges this trust, passing on to the future the "Lamp of Life" whose fire he has been created to guard for a short while.

Immortality, we may point out in passing, is thus no mere hope to the parent: it is a real possibility. The death of the huge agglomeration of highly specialised body-cells is a matter of little consequence, if the germ-plasm, with its power to reproduce not only these body-cells, but the mental traits--indeed, we may in a sense say the very soul-- that inhabited them, has been passed on. The individual continues to live, in his offspring, just as the past lives in him. To the christian, life everlasting is something more than a figure of speech or a theological concept--it is as much a reality as the beat of the heart, the growth of muscles or the activity of the mind. This doctrine of the continuity of germ-plasm throws a fresh light on the nature of human relationships. It is evident that the son who resembles his father cannot accurately be called a "chip off the old block." Rather, they are both chips off the same block; and aside from bringing about the fusion of two distinct strains of germ-plasm, father and mother are no more responsible for endowing the child with its characters except in the choice of mate, than is the child for "stamping his impress" on his parents. From another point of view, it has been said that father and son ought to be thought of as half-brothers by two different mothers, each being the product of the same strain of paternal germ-plasm, but not of the same strain of maternal germ-plasm.

When the respective functions and relative importance, from a genetic point of view, of germ-plasm and body-plasm are understood, it must be fairly evident that the natural point of attack for any attempt at race betterment which aims to be fundamental rather than wholly superficial, must be the germ-plasm rather than the body-plasm. The failure to hold this point of view has been responsible for the disappointing results of much of the sociological theory of the last century, and for the fact that some of the work now carried on under the name of race betterment is producing results that are of little or no significance to true race betterment. On the other hand, it must be fairly evident, from the pains which Nature has taken to arrange for the transmission of the germ-plasm from generation to generation, that she would also protect it from injury with meticulous care. It seems hardly reasonable to suppose that a material of this sort should be exposed, in the higher animals at least, to all the vicissitudes of the environment, and to injury or change from the chance of outward circumstances.

In spite of these presumptions which the biologist would, to say the least, consider worthy of careful investigation, the world is full of well-intentioned people who are anxious to improve the race, and who in their attempts to do so, wholly ignore the germ-plasm. They see only the body-plasm. They are devoted to the dogma that if they can change the body (and what is here said of the body applies equally to the mind) in the direction they wish, this change will in some unascertainable way be reproduced in the next generation. They rarely stop to think that man is an animal, or that the science of biology might conceivably have something to say about the means by which his species can be improved; but if they do, they commonly take refuge, deliberately or unconsciously, in the biology of half a century ago, which still believed that these changes of the body could be so impressed on the germ-plasm as to be continued in the following generation. Such an assumption is made to-day by few who have thoroughly studied the subject. Even those who still believed in what is conventionally called "the inheritance of acquired characteristics" would be quick to repudiate any such application of the doctrine as is commonly made by most of the philanthropists and social workers who are proceeding without seeking the light of biology. But the idea that these modifications are inherited is so widespread among all who have not studied biology, and is so much a part of the tradition of society, that the question must be here examined, before we can proceed confidently with our program of Mendelian inheritance.

The problem is first to be defined. It is evident that all characters which make up a man or woman, or any other organism, must be either germinal or acquired. It is impossible to conceive of any other category. But it is frequently hard to say in which class a given character falls. Worse still, many persons do not even distinguish the two categories accurately--a confusion made easier by the quibble that all characters must be acquired, since the organism starts from a single cell, which possesses practically none of the traits of the adult.

What we mean by an inborn character is one whose expression is due to something which is present in the germ-plasm; one which is inherent and due to heredity. An acquired character is simply a modification, due to some cause external to the germ-plasm acting on an inborn character. In looking at an individual, one cannot always say with certainty which characters are which; but with a little trouble, one can usually reach a reliable decision. It is possible to measure the variation in a given character in a group of parents and their children, in a number of different environments; if the degree of resemblance between parent and offspring is about the same in each case, regardless of the different surroundings in which the children may have been brought up, the character may properly be called germinal. This is the biometric method of investigation. In practice, one can often reach a decision by much simpler means: if the character is one that appears at birth, e.g., skin colour, it is usually safe to assume that it is a germinal character, unless there is some evident reason for deciding otherwise, as in the case of a child born with some disease from which the mother had been suffering for the previous few months. In general, it is more difficult to decide whether a mental trait is germinal, than whether a physical one is; and great care should be used in classification.

To make the distinction, one ought to be familiar with an individual from birth, and to have some knowledge of the conditions to which he was exposed, in the period between conception and birth,--for of course a modification which takes place during that time is as truly an acquired character as one that takes place after parturition. Blindness, for example, may be an inborn defect. The child from conception may have lacked the requisites for the development of sight. On the other hand, it may be an acquired character, due to an ill-advised display of patriotism on July 4, at some time during childhood; or even to infection at the moment of birth. Similarly small size may be an inborn character, due to a small-sized ancestry; but if the child comes of a normal ancestry and is stunted merely because of lack of proper care and food, the smallness is an acquired character. Deafness may be congenital and inborn, or it may be acquired as the result, say, of scarlet fever during childhood. Now the inborn characters (excepting modifications in utero) are admittedly heritable, for inborn characters must exist potentially in the germ-plasm. The belief that acquired characters are also inherited, therefore, involves belief that in some way the trait acquired by the parent is incorporated in the germ-plasm of the parent, to be handed on to the child and reappear in the course of the child's development. The impress on the parental body must in some way be transferred to the parental germ-plasm; and not as a general influence, but as a specific one which can be reproduced by the germ-plasm. This idea was held almost without question by the biologists of the past, from Aristotle on. Questionings indeed arose from time to time, but they were vague and carried no weight, until a generation ago several able men elaborated them. For many years, it was the question of chief dispute in the study of heredity. The last word has not yet been said on it. It has theoretical bearings of immense importance; for our conception of the process of evolution will be shaped according to the belief that acquired characters are or are not inherited. Herbert Spencer went so far as to say, "Close contemplation of the facts impresses me more strongly than ever with two alternatives--either that there has been inheritance of acquired characters, or there has been no evolution." But its practical bearings are no less momentous. Again to quote Spencer: "Considering the width and depth of the effects which the acceptance or non-acceptance of one or the other of these hypotheses must have on our views of life, the question, Which of them is true? Demands beyond all other questions whatever the attention of scientific men. A grave responsibility rests on biologists in respect of the general question, since wrong answers lead, among other effects, to wrong belief about social affairs and to disastrous social actions."

Biologists certainly have not shirked this "grave responsibility" during the last 30 years, and they have, in our opinion, satisfactorily answered the general question. The answer they give is not the answer Herbert Spencer gave.

But the popular mind frequently lags a generation behind, in its grasp of the work of science, and it must be said that in this case the popular mind is still largely under the influence of Herbert Spencer and his school. Whether they know it or not, most people who have not made a particular study of the question still tacitly assume that the acquirements of one generation form part of the inborn heritage of the next, and the present social and educational systems are founded in large part on this false foundation. Most philanthropy starts out unquestioningly with the assumption that by modifying the individual for the better, it will thereby improve the germinal quality of the race.

Even a self-styled truth seeker asks, "Can prospective parents who have thoroughly and systematically disciplined themselves, physically, mentally and morally, transmit to their offspring the traits or tendencies which they have developed?" and answers the question with the astounding statement, "It seems reasonable to suppose that they have this power, it being simply a phase of heredity, the tendency of like to beget like."

The right understanding of this famous problem is therefore fraught with the most important consequences to Mendelian inheritance. The huge mass of experimental evidence that has been accumulated during the last quarter of a century has, necessarily, been almost wholly based on work with plants and lower animals. Even though we cannot attempt to present a general review of this evidence, for which the reader must consult one of the standard works on biology or genetics, we shall point out some of the considerations underlying the problem and its solution.

In the first place, it must be definitely understood that we are dealing only with specific, as distinguished from general, transmission. As the germ-cells derive their nourishment from the body, it is obvious that any cause profoundly affecting the latter might in that way exercise an influence on the germ-cells; that if the parent was starved, the germ-cells might be ill-nourished and the resulting offspring might be weak and puny. There is experimental evidence that this is the case; but that is not the inheritance of an acquired character. If, however, a white man tanned by long exposure to the tropical sun should have children who were brunettes, when the family stock was all blond; or if men whose legs were deformed through falls in childhood should have children whose legs, at birth, appeared deformed in the same manner; then there would be a distinct case of the transmission of an acquired characteristic. "The precise question," as Professor Thomson words it, "is this: Can a structural change in the body, induced by some change in use or disuse, or by a change in surrounding influence, affect the germ-cells in such a specific or representative way that the offspring will through its inheritance exhibit, even in a slight degree, the modification which the parent acquired?" He then lists a number of current misunderstandings, which are so widespread that they deserve to be considered here.

It is frequently argued that unless modifications are inherited, there could be no such thing as evolution. Such pessimism is unwarranted. There is abundant explanation of evolution, in the abundant supply of germinal variations which every individual presents. What is wanted are the facts; each student has a right to interpret them as he sees fit, but not to represent his interpretation as a fact. It is easy to find structural features in Nature which may be interpreted as resulting from the inheritance of acquired characters; but this is not the same as to say and to prove that they have resulted from such inheritance.

It is common to beg the question by pointing to the transmission of some character that is not proved to be a modification. Herbert Spencer cited the prevalence of short-sightedness among the "notoriously studious" Germans as a defect due to the inheritance of an acquired character. But he offered no evidence that this is an acquirement rather than a germinal character. As a fact, there is reason to believe that weakness of the eyes is one of the characteristics of that race, and existed long before the Germans ever became studious--even at a time when most of them could neither read nor write.

The reappearance of a modification may be mistaken for the transmission of a modification. Thus a blond European family moves to the tropics, and the parents become tanned. The children who grow up under the tropical sun are tanned from infancy; and after the grandchildren or great-grandchildren appear, brown from childhood, someone points to the case as an instance of permanent modification of skin-colour. But of course the children at the time of birth are as white as their distant cousins in Europe, and if taken back to the North to be brought up, would be no darker than their kinsmen who had never been in the tropics. Such "evidence" has often been brought forward by careless observers, but can deceive no one who inquires carefully into the facts.

In the case of diseases, re-infection is often mistaken for transmission. The father had pneumonia; the son later developed it; ergo, he must have inherited it. What evidence is there that the son in this case did not get it from an entirely different source? Medical literature is heavily burdened with such spurious evidence.

Changes in the germ-cells along with changes in the body are not relevant to this discussion. The mother's body, for example, is poisoned with alcohol, which is present in large quantities in the blood and therefore might affect the germ-cells directly. If the children subsequently born are consistently defective it is not an inheritance of a body character but the result of a direct modification of the germ-plasm. The inheritance of an acquired modification of the body can only be proved if some particular change made in the parent is inherited as such by the child.

There is often a failure to distinguish between the possible inheritance of a particular modification, and the possible inheritance of indirect results of that modification, or of changes correlated with it. This is a nice but crucial point on which most popular writers are confused. Let us examine it through a hypothetical case. A woman, not herself strong, bears a child that is weak. The woman then goes in for athletics, in order better to fit herself for motherhood; she specialises on tennis. After a few years she bears another child, which is much stronger and better developed than the first. "Look," someone will say, "how the mother has transmitted her acquirement to her offspring." We grant that her improved general health will probably result in a child that is better nourished than the first; but that is a very different thing from heredity. If, however, the mother had played tennis until her right arm was over-developed, and her spine bent; if these characteristics were nowhere present in the ancestry and not seen in the first child; but if the second child were born with a bent spine and a right arm of exaggerated musculature, we would be willing to consider the case on the basis of the inheritance of an acquired character.

Finally, data are frequently presented, which cover only two generations--parent and child. Indeed, almost all the data alleged to show the inheritance of acquired characteristics are of this kind. They are of little or no value as evidence. Cases covering a number of generations, where a cumulative change was visible, would be of weight, but on the rare occasions when they are forthcoming, they can be explained in some other way more satisfactorily than by an appeal to the theory of Lamarck.

If the evidence currently offered to support a belief in the inheritance of acquired characters is tested by the application of these "misunderstandings," it will at once be found that most of it disappears; that it can be thrown out of court without further formality. The Lamarckian doctrine is now held mainly by persons who have either lacked training in the evaluation of evidence, or have never examined critically the assumptions on which they proceed. Medical men and breeders of plants or animals are to a large extent believers in Lamarckism, but the evidence (if any) on which they rely is always susceptible of explanation in a more reasonable way. It must not be forgotten that some of the ablest intellects in the world have been assiduously engaged in getting at the truth in the case, during the last half-century; and it is certainly worthy of consideration that not in a single case has the transmission of an acquired body character ever been proved beyond dispute. Those who still hold a belief in it (and it is fair to say that some men of real ability are among that number) too often do so, it is to be feared, because it is necessary for the support of some theoretical doctrine which they have formulated. Certainly there are few men who can say that they have carefully examined the evidence in the case, and accept Lamarckism because the evidence forces them to do so. It will be interesting to review the various classes of alleged evidence, though we can cite only a few cases from the great number available (most of them, however, dealing with plants or lower animals).

Nearly all the evidence adduced can be put in one of these four classes:

Mutilations.
Diseases.
Results of use or disuse.
Physico-chemical effects of environment.

The case in regard to mutilations is particularly clear cut and leaves little room for doubt. The noses and ears of oriental women have been pierced for generations without number, yet girls are still born with these parts entire. Circumcision offers another test case. The evidence of laboratory experiments (amputation of tails) shows no inheritance. It may be said without hesitation that mutilations are not heritable, no matter how many generations undergo them.

The transmissibility of acquired diseases is a question involved in more of a haze of ignorance and loose thinking. It is particularly frequent to see cases of uterine infection offered as cases of the inheritance of acquired characters. To use the word "heredity" in such a case is unjustified. Uterine infection has no bearing whatever on the question. Taking an historical view, it seems fairly evident that if diseases were really inherited, the race would have been extinct long ago. Of course there are constitutional defects or abnormalities that are in the germ-plasm and are heritable: such is the peculiar inability of the blood to coagulate, which marks "bleeders" (sufferers from hemophilia, a highly hereditary disease). And in many cases it is difficult to distinguish between a real germinal condition of this sort, and an acquired disease.

While there is most decidedly such a thing as the inheritance of a tendency to or lack of resistance to a disease, it is not the result of incidence of the disease on the parent. It is possible to inherit a tendency to headaches or to chronic alcoholism; and it is possible to inherit a lack of resistance to common diseases such as malaria, small-pox or measles; but actually to inherit a zymotic disease as an inherent genetic trait, is impossible,--is, in fact, a contradiction of terms.

When we come to the effects of use and disuse, we reach a much debated ground, and one complicated by the injection of a great deal of biological theorising, as well as the presence of the usual large amount of faulty observation and inference.

It will be admitted by everyone that a part of the body which is much used tends to increase in size, or strength, and similarly that a part which is not used tends to atrophy. It is further found that such changes are progressive in the race, in many cases. Man's brain has steadily increased in size, as he used it more and more; on the other hand, his canine teeth have grown smaller. Can this be regarded as the inheritance of a long continued process of use and disuse? Progressive changes can be satisfactorily accounted for by natural selection; retrogressive changes are susceptible of explanation along similar lines. When an organ is no longer necessary, as the hind legs of a whale, for instance, natural selection no longer keeps it at the point of perfection.

The situation remains the same, when purely mental

processes, such as instincts, are considered. Habit often repeated becomes instinctive, it is said; and then the instinct thus formed by the individual is passed on to his descendants and becomes in the end a racial instinct. Most psychologists have now abandoned this view, which receives no support from investigation. Such prevalence as it still retains seems to be largely due to a confusion of thought brought about by the use of the word "instinctive" in two different senses,--first literally and then figuratively.

Since the importance of hormones (internal secretions) in the body became known, it has often been suggested that their action may furnish the clue to some sort of an inheritance of modifications. The hormone might conceivably modify the germ-plasm but if so, it would more likely be in some wholly different way.

In general, we may confidently say that there is neither theoretical necessity nor adequate experimental proof for belief that the results of use and disuse are inherited.

When we come to consider whether the effects of the environment are inherited, we attack a stronghold of sociologists and historians. Herbert Spencer thought one of the strongest pieces of evidence in this category was to be found in the assimilation of foreigners in the United States. "The descendants of the immigrant Irish," he pointed out, "lose their Celtic aspect and become Americanised.... To say that 'spontaneous variation,' increased by natural selection, can have produced this effect, is going too far." Unfortunately for Mr. Spencer, he was basing his conclusions on guesswork. It is only within the last few months that the first trustworthy evidence on the point has appeared, in the careful measurements of Hrdlička who has demonstrated that Spencer was quite wrong in his statement. As a fact, the original traits persist with almost incredible fidelity.

In 1911, Franz Boas of Columbia University published measurements of the head form of children of immigrants which purported to show that American conditions caused in some mysterious manner a change in the shape of the head. This conclusion in itself would have been striking enough, but was made more startling when he announced that the change worked both ways: "The East European Hebrew, who has a very round head, becomes more long-headed; the south Italian, who in Italy has an exceedingly long head, becomes more short-headed"; and moreover this potent influence was alleged to be a subtle one "which does not affect the young child born abroad and growing up in American environment, but which makes itself felt among the children born in America, even a short time after the arrival of the parents in this country." Boas' work was naturally pleasing to sociologists who believe in the reality of the "melting-pot," and has obtained widespread acceptance in popular literature. It has obtained little acceptance among his fellow-anthropologists, some of whom allege that it is unsound because of the faulty methods by which the measurements were made and the incorrect standards used for comparison.

The many instances quoted by historians, where races have changed after immigration, are to be explained in most cases by natural selection under new conditions, or by interbreeding with the natives, and not as the direct result of climate. Ellsworth Huntington, the most recent and careful student of the effect of climate on man, finds that climate has a great deal of influence on man's energy, but as far as inherited traits in general are concerned, he is constantly led to remark how little heredity is capable of being changed.

Most members of the white race have little toes that are

partly atrophied, and considerably deformed. In many cases one of the joints has undergone ankylosis--that is, the bones have coalesced. It is confidently alleged that this is due to the inheritance of the effects of wearing tight shoes through many centuries. When it is found that the prehistoric Egyptians, who knew not tight shoes, suffered from the same defect in a similar degree, one's confidence in this kind of evidence is much diminished.

The retrogression of the little toe in man is probably to be explained like the degeneration of the hind leg of the whale, as a result of the excess of deteriorating variations which, when not eliminated by natural selection, lead to atrophy. Since man began to limit the use of his feet to walking on the ground, the little toe has had much less value to him.

Breeders are generally of the opinion that good care and feed bestowed on their stock produce results in succeeding generations. This is in a way true, but it is due merely to the fact that the offspring get better nourishment and therefore a better start in life. The changes in breeds, the increase in milk yield, and similar facts, often explained as due to inheritance of acquired characters, are better explained as the results of selection, sometimes conscious, sometimes quite unconscious.

In short, no matter what evidence we examine, we must conclude that inheritance of acquired bodily characters is not a subject that need be reckoned with, in applied Mendelian inheritance.

On the other hand, there is a possible indirect influence of modifications, which may have real importance in man. If the individual is modified in a certain way, in a number of generations, even though such a modification is not transmitted to his descendants, yet its continued existence may make possible, the survival of some germinal variation bearing in the same direction, which without the protecting influence of the pre-existing modification, would have been swamped or destroyed.

Finally, it should be borne in mind that even if physical and mental characters acquired during a man's lifetime are not transmitted, yet there is a sort of transmission of acquired characters which has been of immense importance to the evolution of the race. This is the so-called "inheritance" of the environment; the passing on from one generation to the next of the achievements of the race, its accumulated social experience; its civilisation, in short. It is doubtful whether any useful end is gained by speaking of this continuance of the environment as "heredity;" it certainly tends to confuse many people who are not used to thinking in biological terms. Tradition is the preferable term.

There is much to be said in favour of E. B. Poulton's definition,--"Civilisation in general is the sum of those contrivances which enable human beings to advance independently of heredity." Whatever wisdom, material gain, or language is acquired by one generation may be passed on to the next. As far as the environment is concerned, one generation stands on the shoulders of its predecessor. It might simplify the task of Mendelian inheritance if the same could be said of biological heredity. But it cannot.

In August Weismann's words, the development of a function in offspring begins at the point where it began in his parents, not at the point where it ended in them. Biological improvement of the race (and such improvement greatly fosters all other kinds) must be made through a selective birth-rate. There is no short-cut by way of euthenics, merely.

We must now consider whether there is any direct way of impairing good heredity. It is currently believed that there are certain substances, popularly known as "racial-poisons," which are capable of affecting the germ-plasm adversely and permanently in spite of its isolation and protection. For example, the literature of alcoholism, and much of the literature of Mendelian inheritance, abounds with statements to the effect that alcohol originates degeneracy in the human race. The proof or disproof of this proposition must depend in the last analysis on direct observation and carefully controlled experiments. As the latter cannot be made feasibly on man, a number of students have taken up the problem by using small animals which are easily handled in laboratories. Many of these experiments are so imperfect in method that, when carefully examined, they are found to possess little or no value as evidence on the point here discussed.

Hodge, Mairet and Combemale, for example, have published data which convinced them that the germ-plasm of dogs was injured by the administration of alcohol. The test was the quality of offspring directly produced by the intoxicated animals under experiment. But the number of dogs used was too small to be conclusive, and there was no "control": hence these experiments carry little weight.

Ovize, Fêrê and Stockard have shown that the effect of alcohol on hen's eggs is to produce malformed embryos. This, however, is a case of influencing the development of the individual, rather than the germ-plasm. Evidence is abundant that individual development can be harmed by alcohol, but the experiments with eggs are not to the point of our present purpose.

At the University of Wisconsin, Leon J. Cole has been treating male rabbits with alcohol and reports that "what appear to be decisive results have already been obtained. In the case of alcoholic poisoning of the male the most marked result has been a lessening of his efficiency as a sire, the alcohol apparently having had some effect on the vitality of his spermatozoa." His experiment is properly planned and carried out, but so far as results have been made public, they do not appear to afford conclusive evidence that alcohol originates degeneracy in offspring.

The long-continued and carefully conducted experiment of Charles R. Stockard at the Cornell Medical College is most widely quoted in this connection. He works with guinea-pigs. The animals are intoxicated daily, six days in the week, by inhaling the fumes of alcohol to the point where they show evident signs of its influence; their condition may thus be compared to that of the toper who never gets "dead drunk" but is never entirely sober. Treatment of this sort for a period as long as three years produces no apparent bad effect on the individuals; they continue to grow and become fat and vigorous, taking plenty of food and behaving in a normal manner in every particular. Some of them have been killed from time to time, and all the tissues, including the reproductive glands, have been found perfectly normal. "The treated animals are, therefore, little changed or injured so far as their behaviour and structure goes. Nevertheless, the effects of the treatment are most decidedly indicated by the type of offspring to which they give rise, whether they are mated together or with normal individuals." Before the treatment is begun, every individual is mated at least once, to demonstrate its possibility of giving rise to sound offspring. The crucial test of the influence of alcohol on the germ-cells is, of course, the mating of a previously alcoholised male with a normal, untreated female, in a normal environment.

When the experiment was last reported, it had covered

five years and four generations. The records of 682 offspring produced by 571 matings were tabulated, 164 matings of alcoholised animals, in which either the father, mother, or both were alcoholic, gave 64, or almost 40%, negative results or early abortions, while only 25% of the control matings failed to give full-term litters. Of the 100 full-term litters from alcoholic parents 18% contained stillborn young and only 50% of all the matings resulted in living litters, while 47% of the individuals in the litters of living young died soon after birth. In contrast to this record 73% of the 90 control matings gave living litters and 84% of the young in these litters survived as normal, healthy animals.

We do not minimise the value of this experiment, when we say that too much weight has been popularly placed on its results. Compare it with the experiment with fowls at the University of Maine, which Raymond Pearl reports. He treated 19 fowls with alcohol, little effect on the general health being shown, and none on egg production. From their eggs 234 chicks were produced; the average percentage of fertility of the eggs was diminished but the average percentage of hatch-ability of fertile eggs was increased. The infant mortality of these chicks was smaller than normal, the chicks were heavier when hatched and grew more rapidly than normal afterwards. No deformities were found. "Out of 12 different characters for which we have exact quantitative data, the offspring of treated parents taken as a group are superior to the offspring of untreated parents in 8 characters," in two characters they are inferior and in the remaining two there is no discernible difference. At this stage Dr. Pearl's experiment is admittedly too small, but he is continuing it. As far as reported, it confirms the work of Professor Nice, above mentioned, and shows that what is true for guinea pigs may not be true for other animals, and that the amount of dosage probably also makes a difference. Dr. Pearl explains his results by the hypothesis that the alcohol eliminated the weaker germs in the parents, and allowed only the stronger germs to be used for reproduction.

Despite the unsatisfactory nature of much of the alleged evidence, we must conclude that alcohol, when given in large enough doses, may sometimes affect the germ-plasm of some lower animals in such a way as to deteriorate the quality of their offspring. This effect is probably an "induction," which does not produce a permanent change in the bases of heredity, but will wear away in a generation or two of good surroundings. It must be remembered that although the second-generation treated males of Dr. Stockard's experiment produced defective offspring when mated with females from similarly treated stock, they produced normal offspring when mated with normal females. The significance of this fact has been too little emphasised in writings on "racial poisons." If a normal mate will counteract the influence of a "poisoned" one, it is obvious that the probabilities of danger to any race from this source are much decreased, while if only a small part of the race is affected, and mates at random, the racial damage might be so small that it could hardly be detected.

There are several possible explanations of the fact that injury is found in some experiments but not in others. It may be, as Dr. Pearl thinks, that only weak germs are killed by moderate treatment, and the strong ones are uninjured. And it is probable (this applies more particularly to man) that the body can take care of a certain amount of alcohol without receiving any injury therefrom; it is only when the dosage passes the "danger point" that the possibility of injury appears.

Alcohol has been in use in parts of the world for many centuries; it was common in the Orient before the beginning of historical knowledge. Now if its use by man impairs the germ-plasm, then it seems obvious that the child of one who uses alcohol to a degree sufficient to impair his germ-plasm will tend to be born inferior to his parent. If that child himself is alcoholic, his own offspring will suffer still more, since they must carry the burden of two generations of impairment. Continuing this line of reasoning over a number of generations, in a race where alcohol is freely used by most of the population, one seems unable to escape from the conclusion that the effects of this racial poison, if it be such, must necessarily be cumulative. The damage done to the race must increase in each generation. If the deterioration of the race could be measured, it might even be found to grow in a series of figures representing arithmetical progression.

It seems impossible, with such a state of affairs, that a race in which alcohol was widely used for a long period of time, could avoid extinction. At any rate, the races which have used alcohol longest ought to show great degeneracy--unless there be some regenerative process at work constantly counteracting this cumulative effect of the racial poison in impairing the germ-plasm. Such a proposition at once demands an appeal to history. What is found in examination of the races that have used alcohol the longest? Have they undergone a progressive physical degeneracy, as should be expected?

By no means. In this particular respect they seem to have become stronger rather than weaker, as time went on; that is, they have been less and less injured by alcohol in each century, as far as can be told. Examination of the history of nations which are now comparatively sober, although having access to unlimited quantities of alcohol, shows that at an earlier period in their history, they were notoriously drunken; and the sobriety of a race seems to be proportioned to the length of time in which it has had experience of alcohol. The Mediterranean peoples, who have had abundance of it from the earliest period recorded, are now relatively temperate. One rarely sees a drunkard among them, although many individuals in them would never think of drinking water or any other non-alcoholic beverage. In the northern nations, where the experience of alcohol has been less prolonged, there is still a good deal of drunkenness, although not so much as formerly. But among nations to whom strong alcohol has only recently been made available--the American Indian, for instance, or the Eskimo--drunkenness is frequent wherever the protecting arm of government does not interfere.

What bearing does this have on the theory of racial poisons? Surely a consideration of the principle of natural selection will make it clear that alcohol is acting as an instrument of racial purification through the elimination of weak stocks. It is a drastic sort of purification, which one can hardly view with complacency; but the effect, nevertheless, seems clear cut.

To demonstrate the action of natural selection, we must first demonstrate the existence of variations on which it can act. This is not difficult in the character under consideration--namely, the greater or less capacity of individuals to be attracted by alcohol, to an injurious degree.

As G. Archdall Reid has pointed out, men drink for at least three different reasons: (1) to satisfy thirst. This leads to the use of a light wine or a malt liquor. (2) To gratify the palate. This again usually results in the use of drinks of low alcohol content, in which the flavour is the main consideration. (3) Finally, men drink "to induce those peculiar feelings, those peculiar frames of mind" caused by alcohol.

Although the three motives may and often do coexist in the same individual, or may animate him at different periods of life, the fact remains that they are quite distinct. Thirst and taste do not lead to excessive drinking; and there is good evidence that the degree of concentration and the dosage are important factors in the amount of harm alcohol may do to the individual. The concern of evolutionists, therefore, is with the man who is so constituted that the mental effects of alcohol acting directly on the brain are pleasing, and we must show that there is a congenital variability in this mental quality, among individuals.

Surely an appeal to personal experience will leave little room for doubt on that point. The alcohol question is so hedged about with moral and ethical issues that those who never get drunk, or who perhaps never even "take a drink," are likely to ascribe that line of conduct to superior intelligence and great self-control. As a fact, a dispassionate analysis of the case will show that why many such do not use alcoholic beverages to excess is because intoxication has no charm for them. He is so constituted that the action of alcohol on the brain is distasteful rather than pleasing to him. In other cases it is variation in controlling satisfaction of immediate pleasures for later greater good.

Some of the real inebriates have a strong will and a real desire to be sober, but have a different mental make-up, vividly described by William James: "The craving for drink in real dipsomaniacs, or for opium and chloral in those subjugated, is of a strength of which normal persons can have no conception. 'Were a keg of rum in one corner of the room, and were a cannon constantly discharging balls between me and it, I could not refrain from passing before that cannon in order to get that rum. If a bottle of brandy stood on one hand, and the pit of hell yawned on the other, and I were convinced I should be pushed in as surely as I took one glass, I could not refrain.' Such statements abound in dipsomaniacs' mouths." Between this extreme, and the other of the man who is sickened by a single glass of beer, there are all intermediates.

Now, given an abundant and accessible supply of alcohol to a race, what happens? Those who are not tempted or have adequate control, do not drink to excess; those who are so constituted as to crave the effects of alcohol (once they have experienced them), and who lack the ability to deny themselves the immediate pleasure for the sake of a future gain, seek to renew these pleasures of intoxication at every opportunity; and the well attested result is that they are likely to drink themselves to a premature death.

Although it is a fact that the birth-rate in drunkard's families may be and often is larger than that of the general population, it is none the less a fact that many of the worst drunkards leave no or few offspring. They die of their own excesses at an early age; or their conduct makes them unattractive as mates; or they give so little care to their children that the latter die from neglect, exposure or accident. As these drunkards would tend to hand down their own inborn peculiarity, or weakness for alcohol, to their children, it must be obvious that their death results in a smaller proportion of such persons in the next generation. In other words, natural selection is at work again here, with alcohol as its agent. By killing off the worst drunkards in each generation, nature provides that the following generation shall contain fewer people who lack the power to resist the attraction of the effect of alcohol, or who have a tendency to use it to such an extent as to injure their minds and bodies. And it must be obvious that the speed and efficacy of this ruthless temperance reform movement are proportionate to the abundance and accessibility of the supply of alcohol. Where the supply is ample and available, there is certain to be a relatively high death-rate among those who find it too attractive, and the average of the race therefore is certain to become stronger in this respect with each generation. Such a conclusion can be abundantly justified by an appeal to the history of the Teutonic nations, the nations around the Mediterranean, the Jews, or any race which has been submitted to the test.

There seems hardly room for dispute on the reality of this phase of natural selection. But there is another way in which the process of strengthening the race against the attraction and effect of alcohol may be going on at the same time. If the drug does actually injure the germ-plasm, and set up a deterioration, it is obvious that natural selection is given another point at which to work. The more deteriorated would be eliminated in each generation in competition with the less deteriorated or normal; and the process of racial purification would then go on the more rapidly. The fact that races long submitted to the action of alcohol have become relatively resistant to it, therefore, does not in itself answer the question of whether alcohol injures the human germ-plasm.

Much more observation and measurement must be made before a generalisation can be safely drawn, as to whether alcohol is or is not a racial poison, in the sense in which that expression is used by parents. It has been shown that the evidence which is commonly believed to prove beyond doubt that alcohol does injure the germ-plasm, is mostly worthless. But it must not be thought that the authors intend to deny that alcohol is a racial poison, where the dosage is very heavy and continuous. If we have no good evidence that it is, we equally lack evidence on the other side. We wish only to suggest caution against making rash generalisations on the subject which lack supporting evidence and therefore are a weak basis for propaganda.

So far as immediate action is concerned, Mendelian inheritance must proceed on the basis that there is no proof that alcohol as ordinarily consumed will injure the human germ-plasm. To say this is not in any way to minify the evil results which alcohol often has on the individual, or the disastrous consequences to his offspring, euthenically. But nothing is to be gained by making an assumption of "racial poisoning," and acting on that assumption, without evidence that it is true; and the temperance movement would command more respect from genetics if it ceased to allege proof that alcohol has a directly injurious effect on the race, by poisoning the human germ-plasm, when no adequate proof exists.

How, then, can one account for the immense bulk of cases, some of which come within everyone's range of vision, where alcoholism in the parent is associated with defect in the offspring? By a process of exclusion, we are driven to the explanation already indicated: that alcoholism may be a symptom, rather than a cause, of degeneracy. Some drunkards are drunkards, because they come of a stock that is, in a way, mentally defective; physical defects are frequently correlated in such stocks; naturally the children inherit part or all of the parental defects including, very likely, alcoholism; but the parent's alcoholism, we repeat, must not be considered the cause of the child's defect. The child would have been defective in the same way, regardless of the parent's beverage.

It follows, then, as a practical consequence for Mendelian inheritance, that in the light of present knowledge any campaign against alcoholic liquors would be better based on the very adequate ground of physiology and economics, than on genetics. From the narrowest point of view of genetics, the way to solve the liquor problem would be, not to eliminate drink, but to eliminate the drinker: to prevent the reproduction of the degenerate stocks and the tainted strains that contribute most of the chronic alcoholics. We do not mean to advocate this as the only proper basis for the temperance campaign, because the physiological and economic aspects are of sufficient importance to keep up the campaign at twice the present intensity. But it is desirable to have the Mendelian aspect of the matter clearly understood, and to point out that in checking the production of defectives in the United States, Mendelian inheritance will do its share, and a big share, toward the solution of the drink problem, which is at the same time being attacked along other and equally praiseworthy lines by other people.

The germ-plasm is so carefully isolated and guarded that it is almost impossible to injure it, except by treatment so severe as to kill it altogether; and the degeneracy with which parents are called on to deal is a degeneracy which is running along from generation to generation and which, when once stopped by the cessation of reproduction, is in little danger of being originated anew through some racial poison.

Through these facts, the problem of race betterment is not only immensely simplified, but it is clearly shown to be more a matter for treatment by the biologist, acting through Mendelian inheritance, than for the optimistic improver of the environment.

There is another way in which it is widely believed that some such result as a direct influence of the germ-plasm can be produced: that is through the imaginary process known as maternal impression, prenatal influence, etc. Belief in maternal impressions is no novelty. In the book of Genesis Jacob is described as making use of it to get the better of his tricky father-in-law. Some animal breeders still profess faith in it as a part of their methods of breeding: if they want a black calf, for instance, they will keep a white cow in a black stall, and express perfect confidence that her offspring will resemble midnight darkness. It is easy to see that this method, if it "works," would be a potent instrument for Mendelian inheritance. And it is being recommended for that reason, says a recent writer, who professes on the cover of her book to give a "complete and intelligent summary of all the principles of Mendelian inheritance":

"Too much emphasis cannot be placed upon the necessity of young people making the proper choice of mates in marriage; yet if the production of superior children were dependent upon that one factor, the outlook would be most discouraging to prospective fathers and mothers, for weak traits of character are to be found in all. But when young people learn that by a conscious endeavour to train themselves, they are thereby training their unborn children, they can feel that there is some hope and joy in parentage; that it is something to which they can look forward with delight and even rapture; then they will be inspired to work hard to attain the best and highest that there is in them, leading the lives that will not only be a blessing to themselves, but to their succeeding generation." The author of this quotation has no difficulty in finding supporters. Many physicians and surgeons, who are supposed to be trained in scientific methods of thought, will indorse what she says.

Is there, or is there not, a short cut to race betterment? Everyone interested in the welfare of the race must feel the necessity of getting at the truth in the case; and the truth can be found only by rigorously scientific thought.

Let us turn to the observed facts. This sample is taken

from a little publication which is devoted to Mendelian inheritance. As a "horrible example" the editor gives the case of Jesse Pomeroy, a murderer whom older readers will remember. His father, it appears, worked in a meat market. Before the birth of Jesse, his mother went daily to the shop to carry a luncheon to her husband, and her eyes naturally fell upon the bloody carcases hung about the walls. Inevitably, the sight of such things would produce bloody thoughts in the mind of the unborn child

These are extreme cases; we quote from a medieval medical writer another case that carries the principle to its logical conclusion: A woman saw a Negro,--at that time a rarity in Europe. She immediately had a sickening suspicion that her child would be born with a black skin. To obviate the danger, she had a happy inspiration--she hastened home and washed her body all over with warm water. When the child appeared, his skin was found to be normally white--except between the fingers and toes, where it was black. His mother had failed to wash herself thoroughly in those places

Of course, few of the cases now credited are as gross as this, but the principle involved remains the same. We will take a hypothetical case of a common sort for the sake of clearness: the mother receives a wound on the arm; when her child is born it is found to have a scar of some sort at about the same place on the corresponding arm. Few mothers would fail to see the result of a maternal impression here. But how could this mark have been transmitted? This is not a question of the transmission of acquired characters through the germ-plasm, or anything of that sort, for the child was already formed when the mother was injured. One is obliged, therefore, to believe that the injury was in some way transmitted through the placenta, the only connection between the mother and the unborn child; and that it was then reproduced in some way in the child.

Here is a situation which, examined in the cold light of reason, puts a heavy enough strain on the credulity. Such an influence can reach the embryo only through the blood of the mother. Is it conceivable to any rational human being, that a scar, or what not, on the mother's body can be dissolved in her blood, pass through the placenta into the child's circulation, and then gather itself together into a definite scar on the infant's arm? There is just as much reason to expect the child to grow to resemble the cow on whose milk it is fed after birth, as to expect it to grow to resemble its mother, because of prenatal influence, as the term is customarily used, for once development has begun, the child draws nothing more than nourishment from its mother.

Of course we are accustomed to the pious rejoinder that man must not expect to understand all the mysteries of life; and to hear vague talk about the wonder of wireless telegraphy. But wireless telegraphy is something very definite and tangible--there is little mystery about it. Waves of a given frequency are sent off, and caught by an instrument attuned to the same frequency. How any rational person can support a belief in maternal impressions by such an analogy, if he knows anything about anatomy and physiology, passes comprehension.

Now we are far from declaring that a reason can be found for everything that happens. Science does not refuse belief in an observed fact merely because it is unexplainable. But let us examine this case of maternal impressions a little further. What can be learned of the time element?

Immediately arises the significant fact that most of the marks, deformities and other effects which are credited to prenatal influence must on this hypothesis take place at a comparatively late period in the antenatal life of the child. The mother is frightened by a dog; the child is born with a dog-face. If it be asked when her fright occurred, it is usually found that it was not earlier than the third month, more likely somewhere near the sixth. But it ought to be well known that the development of all the main parts of the body has been completed at the end of the second month. At that time, the mother rarely does more than suspect the coming of the child, and events which she believes to "mark" the child, usually occur after the fourth or fifth month, when the child is substantially formed, and it is impossible that many of the effects supposed to occur could actually occur. Indeed, it is now believed that most errors of development, such as lead to the production of great physical defects, are due to some cause within the embryo itself, and that most of them take place in the first three or four weeks, when the mother is by no means likely to influence the course of embryological development by her mental attitude toward it, for the very good reason that she knows nothing about it. Unless she is immured or isolated from the world, nearly every expectant mother sees many sights of the kind that, according to popular tradition, cause "marks." Why is it that results are so few? Why is it that women doctors and nurses, who are constantly exposed to unpleasant sights, have children that do not differ from those of other mothers?

Darwin, who knew how to think scientifically, saw that this is the logical line of proof or disproof. When Sir Joseph Hooker, the botanist and geologist who was his closest friend, wrote of a supposed case of maternal impression, one of his kinswomen having insisted that a mole which appeared on her child was the effect of fright upon herself for having, before the birth of the child, blotted with sepia a copy of Turner's Liber Studiorum that had been lent her with special injunctions to be careful, Darwin replied: "I should be very much obliged, if at any future or leisure time you could tell me on what you ground your doubtful belief in imagination of a mother affecting her offspring. I have attended to the several statements scattered about, but do not believe in more than accidental coincidences. W. Hunter told my father, then in a lying-in hospital, that in many thousand cases he had asked the mother, before her confinement, whether anything had affected her imagination, and recorded the answers; and absolutely not one case came right, though, when the child was anything remarkable, they afterwards made the cap to fit."

Any doctor who has handled many maternity cases can call to mind instances where every condition was present to perfection, for the production of maternal impression, on the time-honoured lines. None occurred. Most mothers can, if they give the matter careful consideration, duplicate this experience from their own. Why is it that results are so rare? That Darwin gave the true explanation of a great many of the alleged cases is perfectly clear to us. When the child is born with any peculiar characteristic, the mother hunts for some experience in the preceding months that might explain it. If she succeeds in finding any experience of her own at all resembling in its effects the effect which the infant shows, she considers she has proved causation, has established a good case of prenatal influence.

It is not causation; it is coincidence.

If the prospective mother plays or sings a great deal, with the idea of giving her child a musical endowment, and the child actually turns out to have musical talent, the mother at once recalls her yearning that such might be the case; her assiduous practice which she hoped would be of benefit to her child. She immediately decides that it did benefit him, and she becomes a convinced witness to the belief in prenatal culture. Has she not herself demonstrated it? She has not. But if she would examine the child's heredity, she would probably find a taste for music running in the germ-plasm. Her study and practice had not the slightest effect on this hereditary disposition; it is equally certain that the child would have been born with a taste for music if its mother had devoted eight hours a day for nine months to cultivating thoughts of hatred for the musical profession and repugnance for everything that possesses rhythm or harmony.

It necessarily follows, then, that attempts to influence the inherent nature of the child, physically or mentally, through "prenatal culture," are doomed to disappointment. The child develops along the lines of the potentialities which existed in the two germ-cells that united to become its origin. The course of its development cannot be changed in any specific way by any corresponding act or attitude of its mother, good hygiene alone need be her concern.

Indeed, the logical implication of the teaching is the reverse of Mendelian. It would give a woman reason to think she might marry a man whose heredity was most objectionable, and yet, by prenatal culture, save her children from paying the inevitable penalty of this weak heritage. The world has long shuddered over the future of the girl who marries a man to reform him; but think what it means to the future of the race if a superior girl, armed with correspondence school lessons in prenatal culture, marries a man to reform his children

Those who practice this doctrine are doomed to disillusion. The time they spend on prenatal culture is not cultivating the child; it is merely perpetuating a fallacy. Not only is their time thus spent wasted, but worse, for they might have employed it in ways that really would have benefited the child--in open-air exercise, for instance.

To recapitulate, the facts are: That there is, before birth, no connection between mother and child, by which impressions on the mother's mind or body could be transmitted to the child's mind or body. That in most cases the marks or defects whose origin is attribute to maternal impression, must necessarily have been complete long before the incident occurred which the mother, after the child's birth, ascribes as the cause. That these phenomena usually do not occur when they are, and by hypothesis ought to be, expected. The explanations are found after the event, and that is regarded as causation which is really coincidence. Pre-natal care as a euthenic measure is of course not only legitimate but urgent. The embryo derives its entire nourishment from the mother; and its development depends wholly on its supply of nourishment. Anything which affects the supply of nourishment will affect the embryo in a general, not a particular way. If the mother's mental and physical condition be good, the supply of nourishment to the embryo is likely to be good, and development will be normal. If, on the other hand, the mother is constantly harassed by fear or hatred, her physical health will suffer, she will be unable properly to nourish her developing offspring, and it may be its poor physical condition when born, indicates this.

Further, if the mother experiences a great mental or physical shock, it may so upset her health that her child is not properly nourished, its development is arrested, mentally as well as physically, and it is born defective. H. H. Goddard, for example, tells of a high-grade imbecile in the Training School at Vineland, N. J. "Nancy belongs to a thoroughly normal, respectable family. There is nothing to account for the condition unless one accepts the mother's theory. While it sounds somewhat like the discarded theory of maternal impression, yet it is not impossible that the fright and shock which the mother received may have interfered with the nutrition of the unborn child and resulted in the mental defect. The story in brief is as follows. Shortly before this child was born, the mother was compelled to take care of a sister-in-law who was in a similar condition and very ill with convulsions. Our child's mother was many times frightened severely as her sister-in-law was quite out of her mind."

It is easily understandable that any event which makes such an impression on the mother as to affect her health, might so disturb the normal functioning of her body that her child would be badly nourished, or even poisoned. Such facts undoubtedly form the basis on which the airy fabric of prenatal culture was reared by those who lived before the days of scientific biology.

Thus, it is easy enough to see the real explanation of such cases as those mentioned near the beginning of this discussion. The mothers who fret and rebel over their maternity, she found, are likely to bear neurotic children. It is obvious (1) that mothers who fret and rebel are quite likely themselves to be neurotic in constitution, and the child naturally gets its heredity from them: (2) that constant fretting and rebellion would so affect the mother's health that her child would not be properly nourished.

When, however, she goes on to draw the inference that "self-control, cheerfulness and love ... will practically insure you a child normal in physique and nerves," we are obliged to stop. We know that what she says is not true. If the child's heredity is bad, neither self-control, cheerfulness, love, nor anything else known to science, can make that heredity good.

At first thought, one may wish it were otherwise. There is something inspiring in the idea of a mother overcoming the effect of heredity by the sheer force of her own will-power. But perhaps in the long run it is as well; for there are advantages on the other side. It should be a satisfaction to mothers to know that their children will not be marked or injured by untoward events in the antenatal days; that if the child's heredity cannot be changed for the better, neither can it be changed for the worse.

The prenatal culturists and maternal-impressionists are trying to place on her a responsibility which she need not bear. Obviously, it is the mother who is most nearly concerned with the bogy of maternal impressions, and it should make for her peace of mind to know that it is nothing more than a bogy. It is important for the expectant mother to keep herself in as nearly perfect condition as possible, both physically and mentally. Her bodily mechanism will then run smoothly, and the child will get from her blood the nourishment needed for its development. Beyond that there is nothing the mother can do to influence the development of her child.

Now to sum up this long chapter. We started with a consideration of the germ-plasm, the physical basis of life; pointing out that it is continuous from generation to generation, and potentially immortal; that it is carefully isolated and guarded in the body, so that it is not likely to be injured by any ordinary means. One of the logical results of this continuity of the germ-plasm is that modifications of the body of the parent, or acquired characters, can hardly be transferred to the germ-plasm and become a part of the inheritance.

DIFFERENCES AMONG MEN

While Mr. Jefferson, when he wrote into the Declaration of Independence his belief in the self-evidence of the truth that all men are created equal, may have been thinking of legal rights merely, he was expressing an opinion common among philosophers of his time. J. J. Rousseau it was who made the idea popular, and it met with widespread acceptance for many years.

Common enough as applied to mental qualities, the theory of human equality is even more widely held of "moral" qualities. Men are considered to be equally responsible for their conduct, and failure to conform to the accepted code in this respect brings punishment. It is sometimes conceded that men have had differing opportunities to learn the principles of morality; but given equal opportunities, it is almost universally held that failure to follow the principles indicates not inability but unwillingness. In short, public opinion rarely admits that men may differ in their inherent capacity to act morally.

In view of its almost universal and unquestioned, although half unconscious, acceptance as part of the structure of society, it becomes of the utmost importance that this doctrine of human equality should be examined by scientific methods. Fortunately this can be done with ease. Methods of mental and physical measurement that have been evolved during the last few decades offer results that admit of no refutation, and they can be applied in hundreds of different places.

It will not be worthwhile to spend any time demonstrating that all individuals differ, at birth and during their subsequent life, physically. The fact is patent to all. It carries with it as a necessary corollary mental differences,

71

since the brain is part of the body; nevertheless, we shall demonstrate these mental differences independently.

No matter what trait of the individual be chosen, results are analogous. If one takes the simplest traits, to eliminate the most chances for confusion, one finds the same conditions every time. Whether it be speed in marking off all the A's in a printed sheet of capitals, or in putting together the pieces of a puzzle, or in giving a reaction to some certain stimulus, or in making associations between ideas, or drawing figures, or memory for various things, or giving the opposites of words, or discrimination of lifted weights, or success in any one of hundreds of other mental tests, the conclusion is the same. There are wide differences in the abilities of individuals, no two being alike, either mentally or physically, at birth or any time thereafter.

Whenever a large enough number of individuals is tested, these differences arrange themselves in the same general form. It is the form assumed by the distribution of any differences that are governed absolutely by chance. If then, the results of all the tests that have been made on all mental traits be studied, it will be found that human mental ability as shown in at least 95% of all the traits that have been measured, is distributed throughout the race in various degrees, in accordance with the law of chance, and that if one could measure all the members of the species and plot a curve for these measurements, in any trait, he would get this smooth, continuous curve. In other words, human beings are not sharply divided into classes, but the differences between them shade off into each other, although between the best and the worst, in any respect, there is a great gulf.

If this statement applies to simple traits, such as memory for numbers, it must also apply to combinations of simple traits in complex mental processes. For practical purposes, we are therefore justified in saying that in respect of any mental quality,--ability, industry, efficiency, persistence, attentiveness, neatness, honesty, anything you like,--in any large group of people, some individuals will be found who show the character in question in a very low degree, some who show it in a very high degree; and there will be found every possible degree in between.

The consequences of this are significant. Is it desired to eliminate feeble-mindedness? Then it must be borne in mind that there is no sharp distinction between feeble-mindedness and the normal mind. One cannot divide sheep from goats, saying "A is feeble-minded. B is normal. C is feeble-minded. D is normal," and so on. If one took a scale of a hundred numbers, letting 1 stand for an idiot and 100 for a genius, one would find individuals corresponding to every single number on the scale. The only course possible would be a somewhat arbitrary one; say to consider every individual corresponding to a grade under seven as feeble-minded. It would have to be recognised that those graded eight were not much better than those graded seven, but the drawing of the line at seven would be justified on the ground that it had to be drawn somewhere, and seven seemed to be the most satisfactory point.

In practice of course, students of retardation test children by standardised scales. Testing a hundred 10-year-old children, the examiner might find a number who were able to do only those tests which are passed by a normal six-year-old child. He might properly decide to put all who thus showed four years of retardation, in the class of feeble-minded; and he might justifiably decide that those who tested seven years (i.e., three years mental retardation) or less would, for the present, be given the benefit of the doubt, and classed among the possibly normal. Such a procedure, in dealing with intelligence, is necessary and justifiable, but its adoption must not blind students, as it often does, to the fact that the distinction made is an arbitrary one, and that there is no more a hard and fast line of demarcation between imbeciles and normal than there is between "rich men" and "poor men."

The investigation in this direction need not be pursued any farther. For the purpose of Mendelian inheritance, it is sufficient to recognise that great differences exist between men, and women, not only in respect of physical traits, but equally in respect of mental ability.

This conclusion might easily have been reached from a study of the facts in Chapter I, but it seemed worthwhile to take time to present the fact in a more concrete form as the result of actual measurements. The evidence allows no doubt about the existence of considerable mental and physical differences between men.

The question naturally arises, "What is the cause of these differences?"

The study of twins showed that the differences could not be due to differences in training or home surroundings. If the reader will think back over the facts set forth in the first chapter, he will see clearly that the fundamental differences in men cannot be due to anything that happens after they are born; and the facts presented in the second chapter showed that these differences cannot be due in an important degree to any influences acting on the child prior to birth.

Not too much must be expected from vocational guidance at the present time, but in the case of traits that are inherited, it is a fair
inference that a child is more likely to be highly endowed

with a trait which both parents possess, than with one that only one parent possesses. "Among the traits which have been said to occur in some such direct hereditary way," H. L. Hollingworth[164] observes, "or as the result of unexplained mutation or deviation from type, are: mathematical aptitude, ability in drawing,[165] musical composition,[166] singing, poetic reaction, military strategy, chess playing. Pitch discrimination seems to depend on structural factors which are not susceptible of improvement by practice.[167] The same may be said of various forms of professional athletic achievement. Colour blindness seems to be an instance of the conspicuous absence of such a unit characteristic."

Again, the knowledge of ancestry is an essential factor in the wise selection of a husband or wife. Insistence has been laid on this point in an earlier chapter of this book, and it is not necessary here to repeat what was there said. But it seems certain that ancestry will steadily play a larger part in marriage selection in the future; it is
at least necessary to know that one is not marrying into a family that carries the taint of serious hereditary defect, even if one knows nothing more. An intelligent study of genealogy will do much, we believe, to bring about the intelligent selection of the man or woman with whom one is to fall in love.

In addition to these general considerations, it is evident that genealogy, properly carried out, would throw light on most of the
specific problems with which Mendelian inheritance is concerned, or which fall in the field of genetics. A few examples of these problems may be mentioned, in
addition to those which are discussed in various other chapters of this book.

In this connection it is again worth noting that a really

great man is rarely found in an ancestry devoid of ability. This was pointed out in the first chapter, but is certain to strike the genealogist's attention forcibly. Abraham Lincoln is often quoted as an exception; but more recent studies of his ancestry have shown that he is not really an exception; that, as Ida M. Tarbell says, "So far from his later career being unaccounted for in his origin and early history, it is as fully accounted for as is the case of any man." The Lincoln family was one of the best in America, and while Abraham's own father was an eccentric person, he was yet a man of considerable force of character, by no means the "poor white trash" which he is often represented to have been. The Hanks family, to which the Emancipator's mother belonged, had also maintained a high level of ability in every generation; furthermore, Thomas Lincoln and Nancy Hanks, the parents of Abraham Lincoln, were first cousins.

One may also look to one of the greatest characters from history, Alexander III of Macedon, known as the Great. Alexander was the son of Philip II, a man noted for his military genius and natural strength, and Olympias a Epirus princess, wild, visionary and terrible. Is it any wonder to the Mendelian Scientist that Alexander went on to become one of the most celebrated military visionaries of all time.

Charles Dickens the son of John and Elizabeth Dickens, is another such case, Elizabeth being described as having "an inordinate sense of the ludicrous, and remarkable powers of comic mimicry, cheerful, sweet-tempered, and well educated" while his father John was a journalist, and in 1828 a parliamentary reporter. The characteristics of his parents are evident in his success in life.

The more difficult cases, are rather to be found in such ancestries as those of Louis Pasteur and Michael Faraday.

Pasteur might perhaps be justly considered the greatest man France has ever produced; his father was a non-commissioned soldier who came of a long line of tanners, while his mother's family had been gardeners for generations.

Faraday, who is worthy to be placed close to Charles Darwin among eminent Englishmen, was the son of a blacksmith and a farmer's daughter. Such pedigrees are striking; and yet, as Frederick Adams Woods has remarked, they ought to strengthen rather than to weaken one's belief in the force of heredity. When it is considered how rarely such an ancestry produces a great man, it must be fairly evident that his greatness is due to an accidental conjunction of favourable traits, as the modern theory of genetics holds; and that greatness is not due to the inheritance of acquired characters, on which hypothesis Pasteur and Faraday would indeed be difficult to explain.

Cases of this sort, even though involving much less famous people, will be found in almost every genealogy, and add greatly to the interest of its study, as well as offering valuable data.

THE INHERITANCE OF MENTAL CAPACITIES

We have come to the climax of the preliminary argument; if the main differences between human beings are not due to anything in the environment or training, either of this or previous generations, there can be but one explanation for them.

They must be due to the ancestry of the individual--that is, they must be matters of heredity in the ordinary sense, coupled with the fortuitous variations which accompany heredity throughout the organic world. We need not limit ourselves, however, to the argument by exclusion, for it is not difficult to present direct evidence that the differences between men are actually inherited by children from parents. The problem, formally stated, is to measure the amount by which the likeness of individuals of like ancestry surpasses the likeness of individuals of different ancestry. After subtraction of the necessary amount for the greater likeness in training, that the individuals of like ancestry will have, whatever amount is left will necessarily, represent the actual inheritance of the child from its ancestors--parents, grandparents, and so on.

Obviously, the subtraction for environmental effects is the point at which a mistake is most probable. We may safely start, therefore, with a problem in which no subtraction whatever need be made for this cause. Eye colour is a stock example, and a good one, for it is not conceivable that home environment or training would cause a change in the colour of brothers' eyes.

The correlation between brothers, or sisters, or brothers and sisters--briefly, the fraternal resemblance--for eye-colour was found by Karl Pearson, using the method described in Chapter I, to be .52. We are in no danger of contradiction if we state with positiveness that this figure represents the influence of ancestry, or direct inheritance, in respect to this particular trait.

If any well-marked physical character be measured, in which training and environment cannot be assumed to have had any part, it will be found, in a large enough number of subjects, that the resemblance, measured on a scale from 0 to 1, is just about one-half of unity. Of course, perfect identity with the parents is not to be expected, because the child must inherit from both parents, who in turn each inherited from two parents, and so on.

So far, it may be said, we have had plain sailing because we have carefully chosen traits in which we were not obliged to make any subtraction whatever for the influence of training. But it is evident that not all traits fall in that class.

This is the point at which the inheritance of mental traits has been most often questioned. Probably no one will care to dispute the inheritance of such physical traits as eye-colour. But in considering the mind, a certain school of popular pseudo-psychological writers question the reality of mental inheritance, and allege that the proofs which the geneticist offers are worthless because they do not make account of the similarity in environment or training. Of course, it is admitted that some sort of a mental groundwork must be inherited, but extremists allege that this is little more than a clean slate on which the environment, particularly during the early years of childhood, writes its autograph.

We must grant that the analysis of the inheritance of mental traits is proceeding slowly. This is not the fault of the geneticist, but rather of the psychologist, who has not yet been able to furnish the geneticist with the description of definite traits of such a character as to make possible the exhaustive analysis of their individual inheritance.

We might even admit that no inherited "unit character" in the mind has yet been isolated; but it would be a great mistake to assume from this admission that proof of the inheritance of mental qualities, in general, is lacking. The psychologists and educators who think so appear either to be swayed by metaphysical views of the mind, or else to believe that resemblance between parent and offspring is the only evidence of inheritance that can be offered.

The evidence is of numerous kinds, and several lines might be destroyed without impairing the validity of the remainder. It is impossible to review the whole body of evidence here, but some of the various kinds may be indicated, and samples given, even though this involves the necessity of repeating some things we have said in earlier chapters. The reader will then be able to form his own opinion as to whether the geneticists' proofs or the mere assurances of those who have not studied the subject are the more weighty.

The analogy from breeding experiments. Tame rats, for instance, are very docile; their offspring can be handled without a bit of trouble. The wild rat, on the other hand, is not at all docile.

E. Castle, of Harvard University, writes: "We have repeatedly mated tame female rats with wild males, the mothers being removed to isolated cages before the birth of the young. These young which had never seen or been near their father were very wild in disposition in every case. The observations of Yerkes on such rats raised by us indicates that their wildness was not quite as extreme as that of the pure wild rat but closely approached it." Who can suggest any plausible explanation of their conduct, save that they inherited a certain temperament from their sire? Yet the inheritance of temperament is one of the things which certain psychologists most "view with alarm." If it is proved in other animals, can it be considered wholly impossible in man?

If mental defects are inherited, then it is worth while investigating whether mental excellence may also be.

The persistence of like qualities regardless of difference in environment. Any parent with open eyes must see this in his own children--must see that they retained the inherited traits even when they left home and lived under entirely different surroundings. But the histories of twins furnish the most graphic evidence. Galton, who collected detailed histories of thirty-five pairs of twins who were closely alike at birth, and examined their history in after years, writes: "In some cases the resemblance of body and mind had continued unaltered up to old age, notwithstanding very different conditions of life;" in other cases where some dissimilarity developed, it could be traced to the influence of an illness. Making due allowance for the influence of illness, yet "instances do exist of an apparently thorough similarity of nature, in which such differences of external circumstances as may be consistent with the ordinary conditions of the same social rank and country do not create dissimilarity. Positive evidence, such as this, cannot be outweighed by any amount of negative evidence."

Frederick Adams Woods has brought forward a piece of more exact evidence under this head. It is known from many quantitative studies that in physical heredity, the influence of the paternal grandparents and the influence of the maternal grandparents is equal; on the average one pair will contribute no more to the grandchildren than the other. If mental qualities are due rather to early surroundings than to actual inheritance, this equality of

grandparental influence is incredible in
the royal families where Dr. Woods got his material; for
the grandchild has been brought up at the court of the
paternal grandfather, where he ought to have gotten all his
"acquirements," and has perhaps never even seen his
maternal grandparents, who therefore could not be
expected to
impress their mental peculiarities on him by "contagion."
When Dr. Woods actually measured the extent of
resemblance to the two sets of grandparents, for mental
and moral qualities, he found it to be the same in each
case; as is inevitable if they are inherited, but as is
incomprehensible if heredity is not largely responsible for
one's mental make-up.

*Persistence of unlike qualities regardless of sameness in the
environment.* This is the converse of the preceding
proposition, but even more convincing. In the last
paragraph but one, we mentioned Galton's study (cited at
some length in our Chapter I) of "identical" twins, who are
so much alike at birth for the very good reason that they
have identical heredity. This heredity was found to be not
modified, either in the body or the mind, by ordinary
differences of training and environment. Some of Galton's
histories of ordinary, non-identical twins are also given:

One parent says: "They have been treated exactly alike;
both were brought up by hand; they have been under the
same nurse and governess from their birth, and they are
very fond of each other. Their increasing dissimilarity must
be ascribed to a natural difference of mind and character,
as there has been nothing in their treatment to account for
it."

Another writes: "This case is, I should think, somewhat
remarkable for dissimilarity in physique as well as for
strong contrast in character. They have been unlike in

mind and body throughout their lives. Both were reared in a country house and both were at the same schools until the age of 16."

In the face of such examples, can anyone maintain that differences in mental make-up are wholly due to different influences during childhood, and not at all to differences in germinal make-up? It is not necessary to depend, under this head, on mere descriptions, for accurate measurements are available to demonstrate the point. If the environment creates the mental nature, then ordinary brothers, not more than four or five years apart in age, ought to be about as closely similar to each other as identical twins are to each other; for the family influences in each case are practically the same. Professor Thorndike, by careful mental tests, showed that this is not true. The ordinary brothers come from different egg-cells, and, as is known from studies on lower animals, they do not get exactly the same inheritance from their parents; they show, therefore, considerable differences in their psychic natures. Real identical twins, being two halves of the same egg-cell, have the same heredity, and their natures are therefore much more nearly identical.

Again, if the mind is moulded during the "plastic years of childhood," children ought to become more alike, the longer they are together. Twins who were unlike at birth ought to resemble each other more closely at 14 than they did at 9, since they have been for five additional years subjected to this supposedly potent but very mystical "moulding force." Here again Professor Thorndike's exact measurements explode the fallacy. They are actually, measurably, less alike at the older age; their inborn natures are developing along predestined lines, with little regard to the identity of their surroundings. Heredity accounts easily for these facts, but they cannot be squared with the idea that mental differences are the products solely of early training.

Differential rates of increase in qualities subject to much training. If the mind is formed by training, then brothers ought to be more alike in qualities which have been subject to little or no training. Professor Thorndike's measurements on this point show the reverse to be true. The likeness of various traits is determined by heredity, and brothers may be more unlike in traits which have been subjected to a large and equal amount of training. Twins were found to be less alike in their ability at addition and multiplication, in which the schools had been training them for some years, than they were in ability to mark off the A's on a printed sheet, or to write the opposites to a list of words--feats which they had probably never before tried to do.

This same proposition may be put on a broader basis. "In so far as the differences in achievement found amongst a group of men are due to the differences in the quantity and quality of training which they had had in the function in question, the provision of equal amounts of the same sort of training for all individuals in the group should act to reduce the differences." "If the addition of equal amounts of practice does not reduce the differences found amongst men, those differences cannot well be explained to any large extent by supposing them to have been due to corresponding differences in amount of previous practice. If, that is, inequalities in achievement are not reduced by equalising practice, they cannot well have been caused by inequalities in previous practice. If differences in opportunity cause the differences men display, making opportunity more nearly equal for all, by adding equal amounts to it in each case should make the differences less.

"The facts found are rather startling. Equalising practice seems to increase differences. The superior man seems to have got his present superiority by his own nature rather than by superior advantages of the past, since, during a period of equal advantage for all, he increases his lead." This point has been tested by such simple devices as mental multiplication, addition, marking A's on a printed sheet of capitals and the like; all the contestants made some gain in efficiency, but those who were superior at the start were proportionately farther ahead than ever at the end. This is what the geneticist would expect, but fits very ill with some popular pseudo-science which denies that any child is mentally limited by nature.

Direct measurement of the amount of resemblance of mental traits in brothers and sisters. It is manifestly impossible to assume that early training, or parental behaviour, or anything of the sort, can have influenced very markedly the child's eye colour, or the length of his forearm, or the ratio of the breadth of his head to its length. A measure of the amount of resemblance between two brothers in such traits may very confidently be said to represent the influence of heredity; one can feel no doubt that the child inherits his eye-colour and other physical traits of that kind from his parents. It will be recalled that the resemblance, measured on a scale from 0 to 1, has been found to be about 0.5. Karl Pearson measured the resemblance between brothers and sisters in mental traits--for example, temper, conscientiousness, introspection, vivacity--and found it on the average to have the same intensity—that is, about 0.5. Starch gets similar results in studying school grades. Professor Pearson writes: "It has been suggested that this resemblance in the psychological characters is compounded of two factors, inheritance on the one hand and training and environment on the other. If so, one must admit that inheritance and environment make up the resemblance in the physical characters. Now these two sorts of resemblance being of the same intensity, either the environmental influence is the same in both cases or it is not. If it is the same, we are forced to the conclusion that it is insensible, for it cannot influence eye-colour. If it is not the same, then it would be a most marvellous thing that with varying degrees of inheritance, some mysterious force always modifies the extent of home influence, until the resemblance of brothers and sisters is brought sensibly up to the same intensity Occam's razor will enable us at once to cut off such a theory. We are forced, I think, literally forced, to the general conclusion that the physical and psychical characters in man are inherited within broad lines in the same manner, and with approximate intensity. The average parental influence is in itself largely a result of the heritage of the stock and not an extraneous and additional factor causing the resemblance between children from the same home."

A paragraph from Edgar Schuster may appropriately be added. "After considering the published evidence a word must be said of facts which most people may collect for themselves. They are difficult to record, but are perhaps more convincing than any quantity of statistics. If one knows well several members of a family, one is bound to see in them likenesses with regard to mental traits, both large and small, which may sometimes be accounted for by example on the one hand or unconscious imitation on the other, but are often quite inexplicable on any other theory than heredity. It is difficult to understand how the inheritance of mental capacity can be denied by those whose eyes are open and whose minds are open too."

Strictly speaking, it is of course true that man inherits nothing more than the capacity of making mental acquirements. But this general capacity is made up of many separate capacities, all of these capacities are variable, and the variations are inherited. Such seems to us to be the unmistakable verdict of the evidence.

Our conclusions as to the inheritance of all sorts of mental capacity are not based on the mere presence of the same trait in parent and child. As the psychological analysis of individual traits proceeds, it will be possible to proceed further with the study of the inheritance of these traits. Some work has been done on spelling, which is particularly interesting because most people, without reflection, would take it for granted that a child's spelling ability depends almost wholly on his training. Professor Thorndike's exposition of the investigation is as follows:

"E. L. Earle ('03) measured the spelling abilities of some 800 children in the St. Xavier school in New York by careful tests. As the children in this school commonly enter at a very early age, and as the staff and methods of teaching remain very constant, we have in the case of the 180 pairs of brothers and sisters included in the 600 children closely similar school training. Mr. Earle measured the ability of any individual by his deviation from the average for his grade and sex, and found the coefficient of correlation between children of the same family to be .50. That is, any individual is on the average 50% as much above or below the average for his age and sex as his brother or sister.

"Similarities of home training might account for this, but any one experienced in teaching will hesitate to attribute much efficacy to such similarities. Bad spellers remain bad spellers though their teachers change. Moreover, Dr. J. M. Rice in his exhaustive study of spelling ability ('97) found little or no relationship between good spelling and any one of the popular methods, and little or none between poor spelling and foreign parentage. Cornman's more careful study of spelling ('07) supports the view that ability to spell is little influenced by such differences in school or home training as commonly exist."

This is a very clear-cut case of a definite intellectual ability, differences in which might be supposed to be due almost wholly to the child's training, but which seem, on investigation, to be largely due to heredity.

Galton, in his pioneer studies, sought for data on this question. In regard to English judges, he wrote: "Do the judges often have sons who succeed in the same career, where success would have been impossible if they had not been gifted with the special qualities of their fathers?

Out of the 286 judges, more than one in every nine of them have been either father, son or brother to another judge, and the other high legal relationships have been even more numerous. There cannot, then, remain a doubt but that the peculiar type of ability that is necessary to a judge is often transmitted by descent." Galton similarly showed that the sons of statesmen tended to be statesmen, and that the same was true in families of great commanders, literary men, poets and divines. In his list of eminent painters, all the relatives mentioned are painters save four, two of whom were gifted in sculpture, one in music and one in embroidery. As to musicians, Mendelssohn and Meyerbeer are the only ones in his list whose eminent kinsmen achieved their success in other careers than music.

To sum up, we have reason to believe not only that one's mental character is due largely to heredity, but that the details of it may be equally due to heredity, in the sense that for any particular trait or complex in the child there is likely to be found a similar trait or complex in the ancestry. Such a conclusion should not be pushed to the point of assuming inheritance of all sorts of dispositions that might be due to early training; on the other hand, a survey of the whole field would probably justify us in concluding that any given trait is more likely than not to be inherited. The effect of training in the formation of the child's mental character is certainly much less than is popularly supposed;

and even for the traits that are most due to training, it must never be forgotten that there are inherited mental bases.

If the reader has accepted the facts presented in this chapter, and our inferences from the facts, they will admit that mental differences between men & women are at bottom due to heredity, just as physical differences are; that they are apparently inherited in the same manner and in approximately the same degree.

CONSIDERATIONS & NOTES

Career Choices. In addition to their importance to society, a knowledge of the traits of a donor has a great direct importance to the individual; one of the most valuable things to be learned from that knowledge is the answer to the question, "What shall a boy or girl do? What career shall one lay out for one's children?" A knowledge of the child's inborn nature, such as can be had only through study of his ancestry, will guide those who have his education in hand, and will further guide those who decide, or help the child decide, what work to take up in life. This helps to put the problem of vocational guidance on a sound basis,--the basis of the individual's inherent aptitudes.

The choice of a life partner is to be Mendelian. The preferences of 115 young women at Brigham Young College, Logan, Utah. This is a "Mormon" institution and the students, mostly farmers' daughters, are probably expressing ideals which have been very little affected by the demoralising influences of modern city life. The editor of the college paper relates that:

Eighty-six per cent of the girls specifically stated that the young man must be morally pure; 14% did not specifically state.

Ninety-nine per cent specifically stated that he must be mentally and physically strong.

Ninety-three per cent stated that he must absolutely not smoke, chew, or drink; 7% did not state.

Twenty per cent named an occupation they would like the young man
to follow, and these fell into three different classes, that of

farmer, doctor and business.

Four and seven-tenths per cent of the 20% named farmer; 2.7% named doctor, and 1.7% named business man; 80% did not state any profession.

Thirty-three and one-third per cent specifically stated that he must be ambitious; 66-2/3% did not state.

Eight per cent stated specifically that he must have high ideals.

Fifty-two per cent demanded that he be of the same religious conviction; 48% said nothing about religion.

Seventy-two per cent said nothing regarding money matters; 28% stated what his financial condition must be, but none named a specific amount. One-half of the 28% stated that he must be rich, and three-fourths of these were under twenty years of age; the
other half of the 28% said that he must have a moderate income and two-thirds of these were under twenty years of age.

Forty-five per cent stated that the young man must be taller than they; 55% did not state.

Twenty per cent stated that the young man must be older, and from two to eight years older; 80% did not state.

Fifty per cent stated that he must have a good education; one-fourth of the 50% stated that he must have a college education; 95% of these were under twenty-one years of age; 50% did not state his intellectual attainments.

Ninety-one per cent of all the ideals handed in were written by persons under twenty years of age; the other 8-

1/2% were over twenty years of age.

It will not be out of place here to point out that a change in the social valuation of reputability and honour is greatly needed for the
better working of donor selection. The conspicuous waste and leisure that Thorstein Veblen points out as the chief criterion of reputability
at present have a dubious relation to high mental or moral endowment, far less than has wealth. There is much left to be done to achieve a meritorious distribution of wealth. The fact that the insignia of
success are too often awarded to trickery, callousness and luck does not argue for the abolition altogether of the financial success element in reputability, in favour of a "dead level" of equality such as would
result from the application of certain communistic ideals. Distinctions, rightly awarded, are an aid, not a hindrance to sexual selection, and effort should be directed, from the Mendelian point of view, no less to
the proper recognition of true superiority than to the elimination of unjustified differentiations of reputability.

This leads to the consideration of moral standards, and here again details are complex but the broad outlines clear. It seems probable that morality is to a considerable extent a matter of heredity, and the care of the potential mother should be to work with every force that makes for a clear understanding of the moral factors of the world, and to work against every force that tends to confuse the issues. When the issue is clear cut, most people will by instinct tend to marry into moral rather than immoral stocks.

True quality, then, should be emphasised at the expense of false standards. Money, social status, family alignment, though indicators to some degree, must not be taken too much at their face value. Emphasis is to be placed on real

merit as shown by achievement, or on descent from the meritoriously eminent, whether or not such eminence has led to the accumulation of a family fortune and inclusion in an exclusive social
set. In this respect, it is important that the value of a high average
of ancestry should be realised. A single case of eminence in a pedigree should not weigh too heavily. When it is remembered that statistically one grandparent counts for less than one-sixteenth in the heredity of an individual, it will be obvious that the individual whose sole claim to
consideration is a distinguished grandfather, is not necessarily a matrimonial prize. A general high level of morality and mentality in a family is much more advantageous, from the Mendelian point of view, than one "lion" several generations back.

The desirability of selecting a donor from a family of more than one or two children was emphasised by Benjamin Franklin, and is also one of the time-honoured traditions of the Arabs, who have always looked at Mendelian inheritance in a very practical, if somewhat cold-blooded way. It has two advantages: in the first place, one can get a better idea of
what the individual really is, by examining sisters and brothers; and in the second place, there will be less danger of a childless marriage, since it is already proved that the individual comes of a fertile stock.
Francis Galton showed clearly the havoc wrought in the English peerage, by marriages with heiresses (an heiress there being nearly always an only child). Such women were childless in a much larger proportion than ordinary women.

"Marrying a man to reform him" is a speculation in which many women have indulged and usually--it may be said without fear of contradiction--with unfortunate results. It

is always likely that she will fail to reform
him; it is certain that she cannot reform his germ-plasm.
Psychologists agree that the character of a man or woman
undergoes little radical change after the age of 25; and we
know that it is largely determined, potentially, when the
individual is born. It is,
therefore, in most cases it is the height of folly to select a
partner with any marked undesirable trait, with the idea
that it will change after a few years.

The churches have been important instruments in this
connection, and the
worth of their services can hardly be over-estimated, as
they tend to bring together young people of similar tastes
and, in general, of a superior character. Such organisations
as the Young People's Society of Christian Endeavour
serve the Mendelian end in a satisfactory way; it is
almost the unanimous opinion of competent observers
that matches "made in the church" turn out well. Some
idea of the importance of the
churches may be gathered from a census which F. O.
George of the University of Pittsburgh made of 75 married
couples of his acquaintance, asking them where they first
met each other. The answers were:

Church   32
School   19
Private home   17
Dance   7
-- 75

These results need not be thought typical of more than a
small part of the country's population, yet they show how
far-reaching the influence of the church may be on sexual
selection. Quite apart from altruistic motives, the churches
might well encourage social affairs where the young people
could meet, because to do so is one of the surest way of
perpetuating the church.

Conclusion. Carefully tracing your ancestry is considered a fine hobby for enthusiasts, but it has not been given the correct attention by anyone who is considering using a sperm donor. Now, with this book and Mendel's Law, we have a light to guide our way. It is worth noting that there are no guarantees when it comes to heredity, and so this book should not be considered an absolute mathematical axiom. But it can be used to make the best choice for our future family and give the best chance of success to the child. Upon meditation, I have found it most interesting to discover that I have inherited much from my great grandfather, but also my natural strength from my grandfather, my creativity, faith and youthful appearance from both my parents and a certain immovable stubbornness from my dear Nan. It is well worth your time to carefully consider all these aspects for your future, and to aim at the truth in this matter and in all others.

Mark Guy Valerius Tyson

Your notes

Mark Tyson is a Warden at St Augustine's Church Pendlebury. A fully qualified and trained Tailor, Mark is noted for his work on classical studies, Victorianism and Mendelian Law. In his spare time he runs MGVT LIMITED, the spiritual successor to William Tyson's (his great grandfather) business.